New Complete Geography Workbook
Fourth edition

Charles Hayes

Gill & Macmillan

Gill & Macmillan
Hume Avenue
Park West
Dublin 12
with associated companies throughout the world
www.gillmacmillan.ie

© Charles Hayes 2009

978 07171 4092 3

Cartoons by Kate Shannon
Print Origination in Ireland by Design Image, Dublin

*The paper used in this book is made from the wood pulp of managed forests.
For every tree felled, at least one tree is planted, thereby renewing natural resources.*

Contents

eTest.ie – what is it?

A revolutionary new website-based testing platform that facilitates a social learning environment for Irish schools. Both students and teachers can use it, either independently or together, to make the whole area of testing easier, more engaging and more productive for all.

Students – do you want to know how well you are doing? Then take an eTest!

At eTest.ie, you can access tests put together by the author of this textbook. You get instant results, so they're a brilliant way to quickly check just how your study or revision is going.

Since each eTest is based on your textbook, if you don't know an answer, you'll find it in your book.

Register now and you can save all of your eTest results to use as a handy revision aid or to simply compare with your friends' results!

Teachers – eTest.ie will engage your students and help them with their revision, while making the jobs of reviewing their progress and homework easier and more convenient for all of you.

Register now to avail of these exciting features:

■ Create tests easily using our pre-set questions OR you can create your own questions

■ Develop your own online learning centre for each class that you teach

■ Keep track of your students' performances

eTest.ie has a wide choice of question types for you to choose from, most of which can be graded automatically, like multiple-choice, jumbled-sentence, matching, ordering and gap-fill exercises. This free resource allows you to create class groups, delivering all the functionality of a VLE (Virtual Learning Environment) with the ease of communication that is brought by social networking.

Layers of the Earth

★ **1** In the spaces provided in Figure 1, name each layer of the earth labelled **A**, **B** and **C**.

d

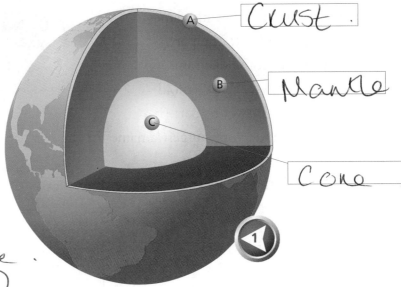

Crust

Mantle

Core

1

2 In relation to Figure 1, indicate whether each of the following statements is true or false (circle the correct *true/false* alternative in each case):

1

(a) The hottest part of   *core* .
    the earth is at **B**.   *True / ~~False~~*

(b) **A** consists of plates which collide with and separate from each other.   *True / False*

why?

Crustal Plates

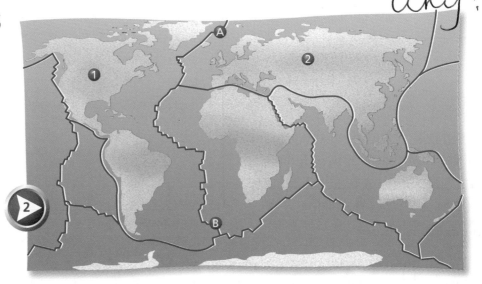

2

★ **3** Examine the map in Figure 2, which shows some of the world's principal crustal plates.

✗ (a) Name the crustal plates labelled **1** and **2**.

    1 _____   2 _____

(b) Name the ocean feature that results from the plates separating along the line labelled **A–B**.

    _____

Folding

★ **4** (a) The rock strata (layers) in the diagram (Figure 3) have been:

pushed together and faulted ☐

pulled apart and folded ☐

pushed together and folded ☐

Tick (✓) the correct box.

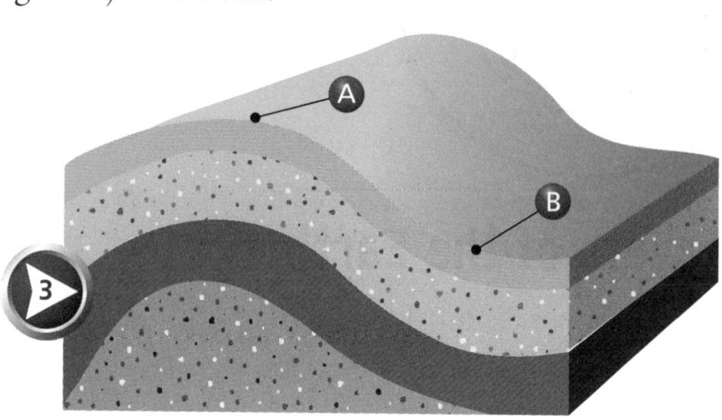

(b) Which of the following names would you give to the part labelled **A** on the diagram?

an upfold ☐   a downfold ☐

(c) Using your answer to part (b) above to guide you, suggest a name for the part labelled **B** in the diagram.

★ **5** Choose one feature associated with **colliding plates**. Describe, with the help of a diagram, how this feature is formed.

Name of feature: _____

How formed: _____

_____

_____

_____

_____

Diagram of feature

6 Photographs **A** and **B** on the page opposite show parts of two different fold mountain ranges: the Andes in South America and the Galty Mountains in Munster.

(a) Which mountains are shown in photograph A? _____

(b) Describe the differences between the Andes and the Galty Mountains under the headings given below.

	Andes	Galty Mountains
Height		
Age		
Foldings in which they originated		

Earthquakes

★ **7** *Earth movements*

Earthquakes and volcanoes often occur:

in Ireland ☐   at the edge of the world's plates ☐

at the centre of the world's plates ☐   in temperate zones ☐

Tick (✓) the correct box.

★ **8** Cross out the **incorrect word** in each of these statements.

Strong earthquakes happen in *Ireland / California*.

Mid-ocean ridges are formed when plates are in *collision / separation*.

Fold mountains are formed when plates are in *collision / separation*.

9 Match each of the terms given below with the correct label in Figure 4.

colliding crustal plates ☐

focus ☐

shock waves and tremors ☐

epicentre ☐

severe damage ☐

less severe damage ☐

10 Name one major result of a strong earthquake.

_____

_____

Some features of an earthquake

③

Volcanic activity

11 The diagram in Figure 5 shows a place where crustal plates separate. Complete the diagram by inserting each of the following labels in the correct boxes:

- *mantle*
- *current of molten rock*
- *plate*
- *place where plates separate*

- *ocean*
- *continent*
- *mid-ocean ridge*
- *volcanic island*

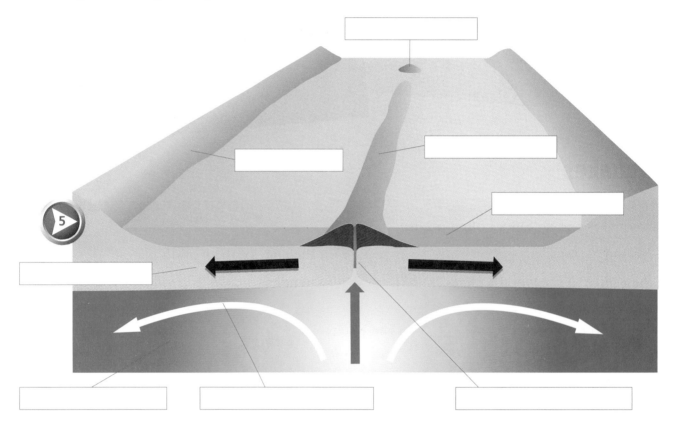

12 The picture shows the island of Surtsey, which is situated in the Atlantic Ocean close to Iceland. Was Surtsey:

formed by folding where plates separated ☐

formed by folding where plates collided ☐

formed by volcanic activity where plates separated ☐

formed by volcanic activity where plates collided ☐

Tick (✓) the correct box.

★ **13** In the boxes provided, name the parts of the volcano indicated by the arrows.

★ **14** The map shows some crustal plates and their boundaries.

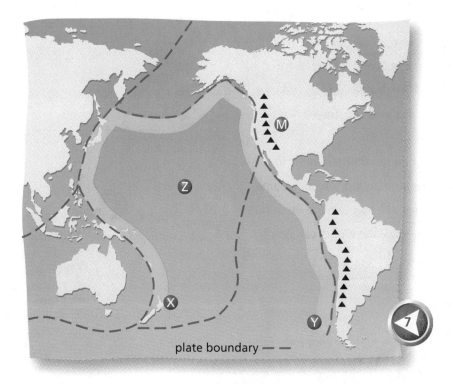

plate boundary — —

Circle the correct answer in **each** of the statements below:

(a) The shaded area labelled **X–Y** is *the Pacific Ring of Fire / the Zone of Ice and Fire.*

(b) The plate labelled **Z** is *the Nazca Plate / the Pacific Plate.*

(c) The mountains labelled **M** are called *the Andes / the Rockies.*

15 Read the news extract in Figure 8 and answer the questions that follow.

Volcanic terror in the Other Emerald Isle

Montserrat – a tiny volcanic island in the Caribbean Sea – is known as 'the other Emerald Isle'. Irish slaves were once shipped here by Oliver Cromwell. They inter-married with black slaves. Their descendants – black people with names like Murphy and O'Flaherty – have become known as 'the black Irish'.

By 1997, Montserrat's 13,500 inhabitants lived quietly in what passing tourists must have thought to be a tiny island paradise.

Then, the local volcano – having been dormant for 350 years – erupted suddenly. In less than a minute, day turned to night as volcanic dust blocked out the sun. People were burned to death when they inhaled red hot ash; while their homes and fields – like a modern Pompeii – were buried in volcanic mud.

When the eruption ended, its terrible cost was counted. Two-thirds of the land and houses were destroyed. Two-thirds of the people were forced into exile. The town of St Patrick's was destroyed completely.

The Caribbean's Emerald Isle now struggles to survive and recover. 'The worst thing,' explained one inhabitant, 'is that we never know when the mountain will erupt again. This Emerald Isle of ours can no longer be trusted fully.'

(a) Which island suffered the 'volcanic terror'?

_____

(b) In which sea is the island situated?

_____

(c) The volcano was once *dormant*. What does that mean?

_____

_____

(d) List three results of the volcanic eruption described.

- _____

    _____

- _____

    _____

- _____

    _____

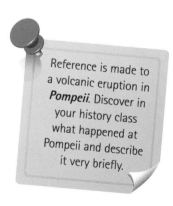

Reference is made to a volcanic eruption in *Pompeii*. Discover in your history class what happened at Pompeii and describe it very briefly.

Funtime!

... for EXTRA fun!

Enjoy this crossword puzzle. Most of the answers are to be found in **Chapter 1** of your **textbook**. But there are a few that you will have to research or puzzle out for yourself ...

Clues Across

1. South American fold mountains.
3. On top of a volcanic mountain.
6. Comes out of volcanoes.
8. African country and mountain.
10. Inside earth but sounds like a cover.
11. Volcanic material or soil and water.
13. Outer part of bread or earth.
14. American city prone to earthquakes.
15. Pipe through which volcano erupts.
18. Volcanic Pacific island, 20°N, 156°W.
19. Cazan – a mixed-up plate.
21. This volcanic country sounds really cool.
22. County/city in Northern Ireland.
23. Crustal plate 'down under'.

Clues Down

1. Volcanic material or burnt-out fuel wood.
2. You cannot eat from these pieces of earth-crust.
3. The planet's centre.
4. Sicilian volcano, or girl's name.
5. Physical features (L A _ D _ O R M S).
7. When the ground trembles.
9. Ireland's crustal plate.
12. Was 6 across before it flows out of a vent.
16. Volcano – dead like Slemish.
17. Beneath the Mid Atlantic.
20. Around the Pacific – a 'Ring of _ _ _ _'.

1 Which of the following types of rock is shown in Figure 1?

metamorphic ☐

igneous ☐

sedimentary ☐

Tick (✓) the correct box.

★

◀ 1 Sandstone

2 Write in the boxes the type of rock (limestone, sandstone, etc.) that is most likely to be found in each of the locations labelled 1–5 on the map in Figure 2.

1	
2	
3	
4	
5	

★ **3** Choose **three** terms from the *selection box* to fill in the spaces in the *extract* below.

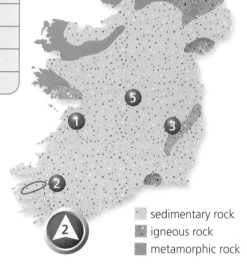

▽ 2

sedimentary rock
igneous rock
metamorphic rock

Selection Box

Metamorphic	Sandstone	Basalt
Quartzite	Shale	Igneous
Marble	Sedimentary	Limestone

Extract

'There are many types of rock in Ireland. These range from regular-shaped columns of _____ in Antrim's Giant's Causeway to multi-coloured granite on the Wicklow Mountains. Both of these rock types are _____, which means they were once formed from hot, volcanic material. The centre of Ireland consists mostly of _____, in which fossils of ancient sea creatures can sometimes be found.'

★ **4** Examine **Picture A** and **Picture B**, which show two different **rock types** in Ireland. Answer the questions that follow.

Picture A – The Giant's Causeway

Picture B – The Burren, Co. Clare

(a) Name the type of rock shown:

in Picture A   _____

in Picture B   _____

(b) Indicate whether each rock type you named is igneous, sedimentary or metamorphic.

in Picture A   _____

in Picture B   _____

(c) Describe two ways in which rocks may be of benefit to people.

(i)   _____

(ii)   _____

★ **5** In the boxes provided, match each letter in Column X with the number of its pair in Column Y. One match has been completed for you.

Column X	
A	Ireland's most common sedimentary rock
B	Metamorphic rock that was once sandstone
C	Igneous rock found at the Giant's Causeway, Co. Antrim
D	Coarse multi-coloured igneous rock found in Wicklow
E	A fossil fuel found in the Midlands of Ireland

Column Y	
1	Quartzite
2	Granite
3	Limestone
4	Basalt
5	Peat

A	3
B	
C	
D	
E	

★ **6** Complete the three-piece crossword using these clues:

1. Coarse red or brown sedimentary rock found in the mountains of Munster.
2. A coarse, multi-coloured igneous rock.
3. Rocks which were changed by great pressure or heat.

★ **7** Imagine a quarry is to be opened near where you live. Explain why some people would be in favour of it **and** why some people would be against it.

Arguments in favour	Arguments against
• _____ _____ _____ • _____ _____ _____ _____	• _____ _____ _____ • _____ _____ _____ _____

Field Study

8 Collect a small sample of a common rock type in your area. Bring the sample to school. Describe the characteristics of this rock (what it looks and feels like). Try to find out what type of rock it is and how it was formed.

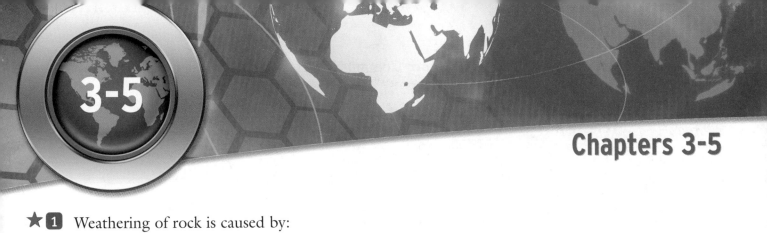

★ **1** Weathering of rock is caused by:

rivers ☐   freezing and thawing ☐

climatic change ☐   volcanic activity ☐

★ **2**

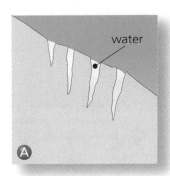

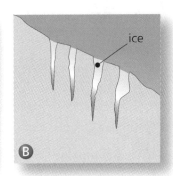

Circle the correct answer in **each** of the statements below.

(a) The process shown in the diagram is *freeze-thaw action / solution*.

(b) This is an example of *chemical / mechanical weathering*.

(c) This process produces *clints and grikes / scree*.

3 Name and describe briefly the **weathering process** that is active in each of the photographs below.

Name: _____

Description: _____

_____

_____

_____

Name: _____

Description: _____

_____

_____

_____

★ **4** In the boxes provided, match each letter in Column X with the number of its pair in Column Y. One pair has been completed for you.

Column X	
A	Granite
B	Running water
C	Moving crustal plates
D	Frost action
E	Deposition on sea floor

Column Y	
1	Igneous
2	Fold mountains
3	Limestone
4	Erosion
5	Weathering

A	1
B	
C	
D	
E	

5 In the grid provided, write the names of each of the features labelled **A-I** in Figure 2.

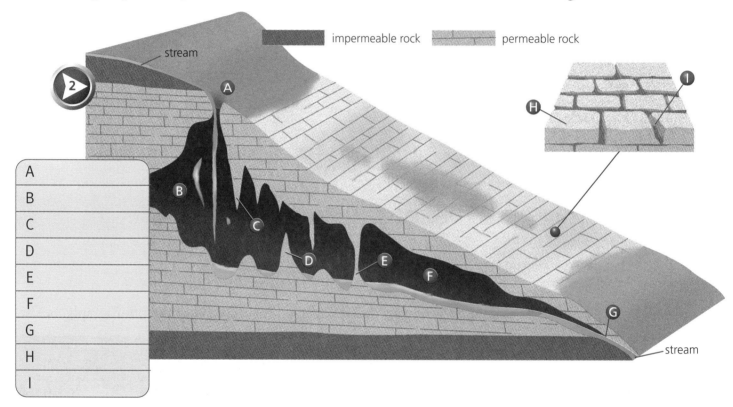

impermeable rock   permeable rock

stream

stream

A	
B	
C	
D	
E	
F	
G	
H	
I	

★ **6** Many tourists visit the wide range of attractions in the Burren. While these tourists bring many *benefits* to the area, they also cause some *problems*. In the spaces below, describe two benefits and two problems of tourism for the Burren.

Benefits	Problems
• _____ _____ • _____ _____	• _____ _____ • _____ _____

Funtime!

This word puzzle is a fun way of testing yourself on the material in Chapters 2 to 5.

Clues Across

1. Might gobble down a river in the Burren.
2. Area of exposed limestone.
3. Visit 1 and 2 above in this county.
4. A soil conditioner processed from limestone.
5. Was limestone before it changed.
6. In some rocks – reacts with carbonic acid.
7. Metamorphic – from sandstone.
8. Rock-embedded remains of plants or animals.
9. Between the grikes in limestone pavement.
10. Underground limestone feature.
11. _ _ _ _ _ _ Causeway.
12. Heaps of frost-weathered rock fragments.

13. Through which water can pass.
14. CO_2 – atmospheric gas.
15. In this part of Leinster you will find 5 across in black.
16. Not mechanical weathering.
17. Rocks formed from volcanic material.
18. A person who studies plants.
19. Layers of rock.
20. An agent of mechanical weathering.
21. Made of Antrim basalt – The Giant's _____.

Clues Down

1. They hang 'tite' from the cave roof!
12. A well-known rock group.

1 In the grid provided, name four types of mass movement and write two sentences to describe each type.

Four types of mass movement	
Name	**Description**
1	
2	
3	
4	

★ **2** (a) What type of mass movement is shown in Figure 1?

_____

(b) How do you know this type of mass movement is taking place? Mention three pieces of evidence shown in Figure 1.

_____

_____

_____

3 The diagrams **A**, **B** and **C** in Figure 2 show how human activities could have contributed to mass movement on the Dart line between Greystones and Bray, Co. Wicklow.

Rail builders cut into steep slope

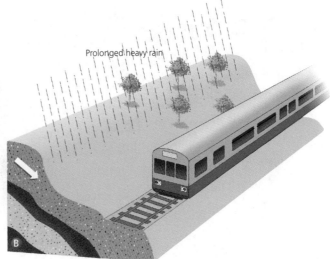

Prolonged heavy rain

(a) Name the type of mass movement shown in diagram C.

_____

(b) With the help of the three diagrams, attempt to explain why this mass movement happened.

_____

_____

_____

_____

_____

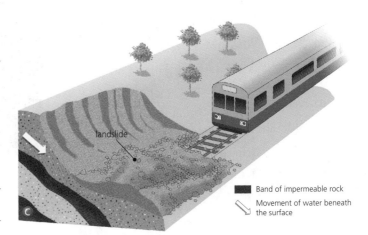

landslide

■ Band of impermeable rock

↘ Movement of water beneath the surface

4 Try to explain each of the following:

● How an earthquake might cause a landslide to happen. _____

_____

_____

● How vegetation might help to prevent mass movement. _____

_____

_____

5 Examine the news extract and photograph relating to **a landslide in Co. Mayo**. Then answer the questions that follow.

NIGHTMARE IN MAYO

One night in September 2003, the people of Pollathomas, Co. Mayo awoke suddenly to a noise like thunder. It was the sound of thousands of tonnes of mud, earth and rock ripping down Duncarton hill in a series of massive landslides.

The landslides tore up roads and destroyed bridges. Farm animals died as farmland was covered in rubble. A local graveyard was devastated and some graves were swept into the sea. One holiday home was completely destroyed and several other holiday homes were seriously damaged. Miraculously, no one was killed.

The landslides were triggered by a period of very heavy rain, which had saturated the hillside and made its soil cover heavy and unstable. There appears to be no evidence that possible overgrazing by sheep or the building of a road on the hillside might have contributed to the disaster.

(a) Where in Co. Mayo did the landslides occur?

_____

(b) List three things mentioned in the news extract that might help cause landslides.

- _____
- _____
- _____

(c) Name five results of the Mayo landslides.

- _____
- _____
- _____
- _____
- _____

6 True or false quiz

Indicate whether each of the following statements is true or false.
Then check the answers given upside-down in the box.

(a) Regolith is loose broken rock on the earth's surface.   _____

(b) Heavy rain provides water that binds the soil
     together and helps to prevent mass movement   _____

(c) An avalanche is the rapid downslope movement of rocks and mud   _____

(d) Deforestation (the clearing of forests) can contribute to mass movement   _____

(e) Soil creep is the slowest form of mass movement and can happen on
     very gentle slopes   _____

(f) Bogbursts involve the downward movement of peat   _____

(g) A mudflow destroyed the village of Panabaj in Columbia   _____

(h) Landslides from Duncarton Hill caused damage in Pollathomas, Co. Mayo   _____

Answers: (a) true; (b) false; (c) false; (d) true; (e) true; (f) true; (g) false; (h) true.

7 Wordwheels

Insert the missing letters to complete the names of two types of mass movement reading either
clockwise or anticlockwise.

1 Use the words in the *selection box* to write the correct term in each of the *blank spaces* in the account below.

Selection Box

- ox-bow lakes
- V-shaped
- Mississippi
- meanders
- waterfall
- Shannon
- levees
- source
- interlocking spurs
- Erne
- United States
- flood plain
- reservoir
- suspended
- expensive
- hurricane
- inside
- Tipperary
- downward
- load
- deltas
- deposition
- old age
- hydroelectricity

The story of a river

The _____ or beginning of a river is usually on high ground. The young river flows through a _____ valley, which it erodes _____. Most erosion is carried out by the material, or _____, which is carried by the river. The course of the young river typically winds its way between _____ _____ and may occasionally descend vertically over a _____.

At its stage of maturity, the river may carry a large load, the lightest particles of which are _____ in the water and may give the river a tea-brown colour. Wide valley floors are now crossed by pronounced _____ or curves in the river. The river usually erodes the outside and deposits on the _____ of a meander.

At its _____ _____ stage, the river meanders slowly towards its mouth. Erosion has now given way to _____, which builds up a wide, flat plain called a _____ _____. Other features of senility or old age include narrow riverside ridges called _____, horseshoe-shaped _____ _____ _____ and – in the case of some rivers – triangular-shaped features called _____.

Rivers such as the _____ and the _____ have been dammed in order to generate _____. The artificial lake or _____ behind the dam can be used also as a valuable fresh water supply. But such lakes often flood valuable farmland and the dams, which create them, are _____ to build.

The flood plains of some 'old' rivers suffer from flooding. In recent years, the River Suir has broken its banks to flood parts of Clonmel in Co. _____. New Orleans in the _____ _____ suffered terrible flooding when a _____ called 'Katrina' caused a surge of water to sweep up the _____ river and break through the levees that protect the city.

2 In the boxes provided, match each letter in the diagram with the number of its pair in Column X. One match has been completed for you.

A	
B	
C	
D	
E	
F	
G	
H	
I	
J	

Column X
1. delta
2. interlocking spurs
3. meander
4. confluence
5. flood plain
6. waterfall
7. source
8. levee
9. ox-bow lake
10. tributary

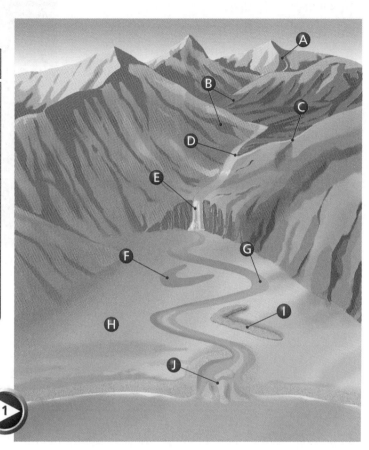

★ **3** The diagrams A, B and C show a river in its upper, middle and lower courses.

Diagram A

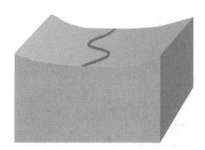

Diagram B

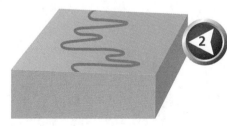

Diagram C

Circle the correct answer in **each** of the statements below:

(a) Sideward erosion is most common in *Diagram A / Diagram B / Diagram C.*

(b) Deposition is most common in *Diagram A / Diagram B / Diagram C.*

(c) Downward erosion is most common in *Diagram A / Diagram B / Diagram C.*

★ **4** (a) The feature shown in Figure 3 is called:

a beach ☐

an esker ☐

a waterfall ☐

a delta ☐

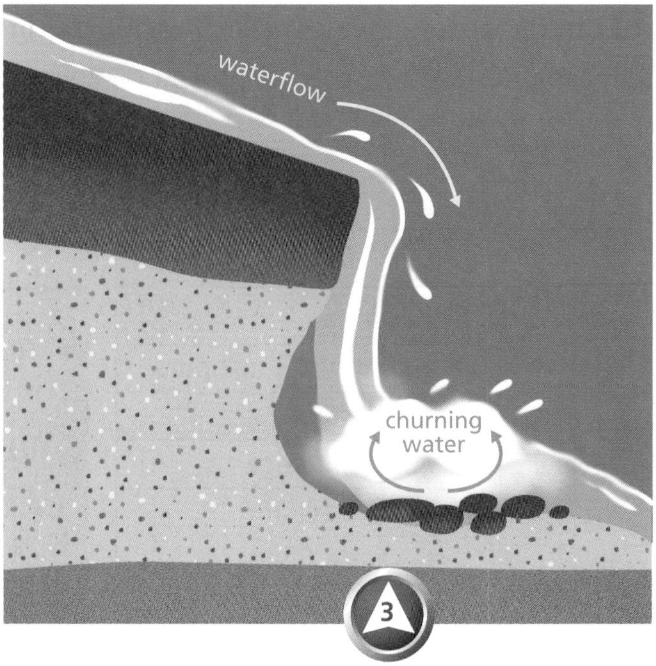

(b) In the space below, describe how the feature in Figure 3 was formed. Name one river in which such a feature can be found.

_____

_____

_____

_____

_____

_____

_____

Example of river: _____

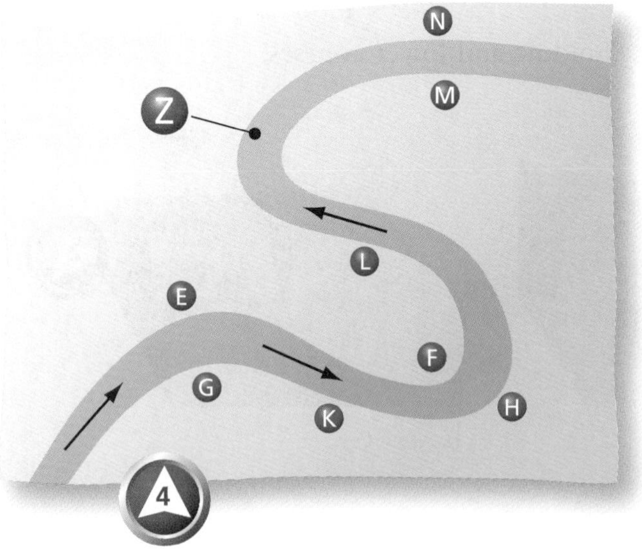

★ **5** (a) Look at Figure 4, which shows part of the course of a river.

The *feature* marked Z is called:

a waterfall ☐

a delta ☐

an estuary ☐

a meander ☐

★ (b) The river is:

eroding at E and depositing at F ☐

eroding at G and depositing at H ☐

eroding at K and depositing at L ☐

eroding at M and depositing at N ☐

Tick (✓) the correct box.

The Great Dam of China

China's Three Gorges Dam is the largest in the world. It is more than two kilometres wide and nearly a fifth of a kilometre high. It holds back the Yangtze, which is the world's third largest river.

Members of the Chinese government are quick to point out the great dam's advantages. It is designed to regulate the flow of the Yangtze, and so prevent flooding. This is important in a region where nearly one million people have been drowned in river floods in the past 100 years. The dam will also provide huge amounts of much-needed and clean hydroelectric power. The project will give coastal shipping better access to the interior of China. The huge reservoir (lake) behind the dam will provide water supplies for countless people and can be used for fish farming.

But the dam also has its critics. The rising waters of the reservoir have flooded millions of hectares of farmland, as well as places of historical interest. Up to two million people have lost their homes and have been sent to live in other areas. Many of these people were farmers, who now find themselves with no useful work.

5

6 Study the newspaper extract and answer the questions below.

(a) Indicate whether each of the following statements is true or false by circling the *true* or *false* option in each case.

   (i) The Three Gorges dam is on the Yangtze River in China. *True / False*

   (ii) The dam is on the world's longest river. *True / False*

   (iii) The dam is nearly one fifth of a kilometre high and more than two kilometres wide. *True / False*

(b) In the spaces provided outline **two advantages** and **two disadvantages** of hydroelectric power (HEP) schemes that are referred to in the above newspaper extract.

Advantages	Disadvantages
• _____	• _____
_____	_____
_____	_____
• _____	• _____
_____	_____
_____	_____

★ **1** In the box provided name the features labelled A to F in Figure 1.

A _____

B _____

C _____

D _____

E _____

F _____

★ **2** Which of the following are **all** landscape features of glacial erosion? *Tick (✓) the correct box.*

(a) Hanging valleys, pyramidal peaks, drumlins, arêtes. ☐

(b) Corries, eskers, hanging valleys, moraines. ☐

(c) Corries, arêtes, glacial valleys, pyramidal peaks. ☐

(d) Moraines, corries, eskers, hanging valleys. ☐

★ **3** In the boxes provided, match each letter in Column X with the number of its pair in Column Y. One pair has been completed for you.

	Column X			Column Y			
A	Corrie	1	Narrow ridge between two corries		A	4
B	Arête	2	Glaciated valley overhanging main valley		B	
C	Fiord	3	Hollow on valley floor scooped out by ice		C	
D	Hanging valley	4	Steep-sided hollow sometimes containing a lake		D	
E	Ribbon lake	5	Glaciated valley drowned by rising sea levels		E	

4 (a) The valley shown in this image has undergone erosion by ice. Name three glacial features in the image that prove that this is so.

1 _____

2 _____

3 _____

(b) Describe the formation of each of the features labelled **A** and **B** on the image.

A _____

_____

_____

_____

B _____

_____

_____

_____

5 Glaciation and people

Write an account of two positive (good) and two negative (bad) effects of glaciation in Ireland.
Use the information on Figure 2 to *help* you, but make up your own answers.

Ice has eroded soil from mountains

Roads use glacial valleys which cut through highlands

Beautiful scenery in glaciated highlands

Glacier deposited many large boulders on valley floor

Poor, marshy land between drumlins

Fertile boulder clay on glaciated lowlands

Roads have to wind between drumlins

Sand and gravel pits in esker

2

Positive effects of glaciation:

1 _____

_____

2 _____

_____

Negative effects of glaciation:

1 _____

_____

2 _____

_____

Chapter 9

1 In the spaces provided in the grid, identify each of the features labelled **A to J** in Figure 1. Indicate whether each feature is formed by erosion or deposition by writing **E** or **D** on the appropriate spaces.

	Feature	E or D
A		
B		
C		
D		
E		
F		
G		
H		
I		
J		

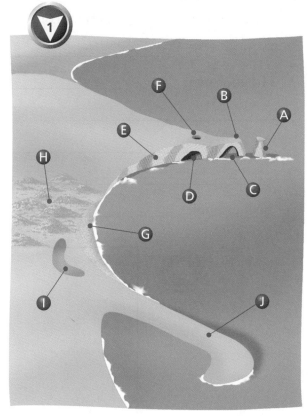

★ **2** In the boxes provided, match each letter in Column X with the number of its pair in Column Y. One pair has been completed for you.

	Column X
A	Lagoon
B	Abrasion
C	Tombolo
D	Longshore drift
E	Sand dune
F	Storm beach
G	Sand spit

	Column Y
1	Links an 'island' to the mainland
2	Bay cut off from the sea by a body of sand
3	Mounds of sand anchored by marram grass
4	Ridge of sand and shingle jutting out into the sea
5	Deposition when waves are very strong
6	Movement of material along a beach
7	Erosion by the load carried by waves

A	
B	
C	1
D	
E	
F	
G	

★**3** Name and describe briefly one way that people use coastal areas and one way that people pollute coastal areas.

Use: _____

_____

Pollute: _____

_____

4 Name one feature of marine (sea) erosion. With the help of a labelled diagram, describe how this feature was formed. Name one Irish example of the feature.

Feature: _____

How formed: _____

_____

_____

_____

Irish example: _____

Labelled diagram
of feature

Funtime!

This monster word game will help you to revise chapters 1 to 9.

Clues Across

2. At the top of a volcanic mountain.
7. Pillar-like feature formed by sea erosion.
8. Often disastrous tremors in the earth's crust.
12. The tidal mouth of a river.
14. 'Land of ice and fire.'
15. One of the three main rock groups.
17. Remains of a plant or animal preserved in rock.
18. Deposits of sand and shingle found between high- and low-tide levels.
19. Limestone area in north Co. Clare.
20. Horseshoe-shaped lake found in river floodplain.
21. Slow-moving river of ice.
24. Feature of sea erosion/underground limestone feature.
25. The slowest form of mass movement.
27. Man-made features built to halt longshore drift.
30. A pronounced bend in a river.
31. Basin-shaped hollow, 'birthplace' of a glacier.
32. Deep cracks in a glacier.

Clues Down

1. Narrow 'pipe' through which volcanic material may reach the earth's surface.
3. Mountains in North America.
4. Between the American and the African crustal plates – the Mid Atlantic _____.
5. Type of metamorphic rock found on the Hill of Howth.
6. A large area of high, flat land.
7. The front of a glacier.
9. Type of sedimentary rock found in Kerry mountains.
10. Sharp ridge between adjacent corries.
11. The Pacific Ring of _____ is a zone of earthquakes and volcanic activity.
13. Feature of sea erosion, a well-known example of which is at the Old Head of Kinsale.
16. Rock fragments resulting from freeze-thaw weathering.
20. Liquid rock and source of energy.
22. Another name for a cirque.
23. The place where a river begins.
26. Moving ice may do this to erode.
28. Feature of sea deposition/sounds rude.
29. Feature of sea deposition/pub.

1 The diagram in Figure 1 illustrates **global warming**. Complete the diagram by selecting labels from the *selection box* and writing them into the boxes labelled **A–F**.

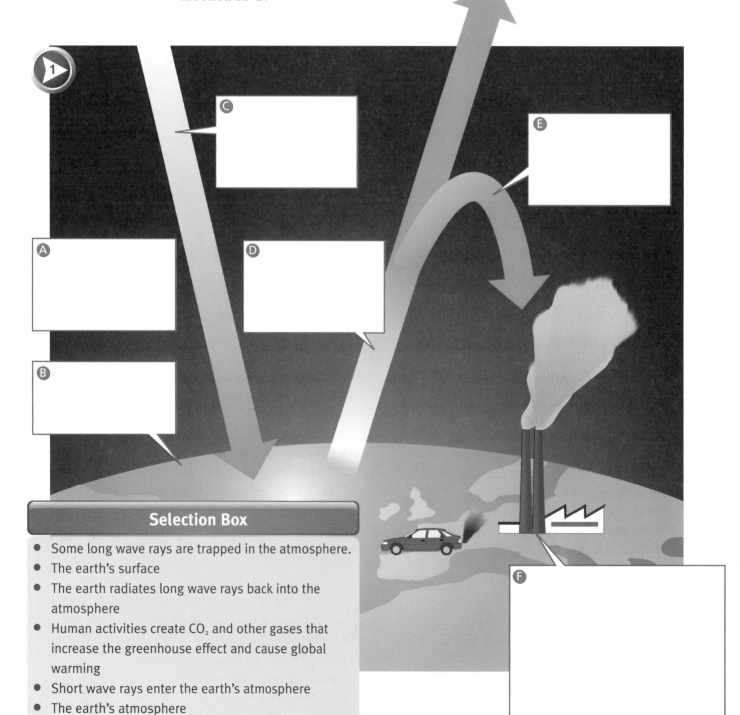

Selection Box

- Some long wave rays are trapped in the atmosphere.
- The earth's surface
- The earth radiates long wave rays back into the atmosphere
- Human activities create CO_2 and other gases that increase the greenhouse effect and cause global warming
- Short wave rays enter the earth's atmosphere
- The earth's atmosphere

★ **2** In the case of each of the following statements, circle the correct alternative.

(a) The major cause of global warming is: *burning fossil fuels / more hydroelectric power stations / more buildings using glass.*

(b) CFCs have an influence on: *the Greenhouse Effect and the ozone layer / acid rain / nuclear power / desertification.*

3 The cartoon in Figure 2 refers to human activities and global warming. The statements below refer to **the messages given by the cartoon**. Not all of the statements are true.

1 SUVs* are a threat to children because they are dangerous to drive.

2 SUVs contribute to global warming.

3 SUVs are a threat to children's future because they damage the environment.

4 People with children buy SUVs.

5 Some people act without thinking of the long term effects of their actions.

The correct statements are numbers: [*Tick ✓ the correct box*]

1, 2, 3	☐	2, 4, 5	☐
2, 3, 5	☐	3, 4, 5	☐

'SUV' stands for 'Sports Utility Vehicle', such as that shown in the cartoon.

4 (a) Figure 3 shows a map of **the ocean currents of the world**. Use the map to answer the following questions.

Circle the correct *alternatives* in each of the following statements.

(i) Ocean currents generally follow *clockwise / anti-clockwise* patterns in the Northern Hemisphere.

(ii) Ocean currents generally flow in a *clockwise / anti-clockwise* pattern south of the equator.

(iii) The clockwise and anti-clockwise patterns of ocean currents is owing to *Storm Force / Coriolis Force*, which is related to the rotation of the earth on its axis from *west to east / east to west*.

(iv) Currents that flow towards the equator are generally called *warm / cold* currents.

(v) The only current that flows around the world without interruption is called the *North Atlantic Drift / West Wind Drift*.

(b) In the grid provided, name each of the ocean currents labelled **1–5** on the map.

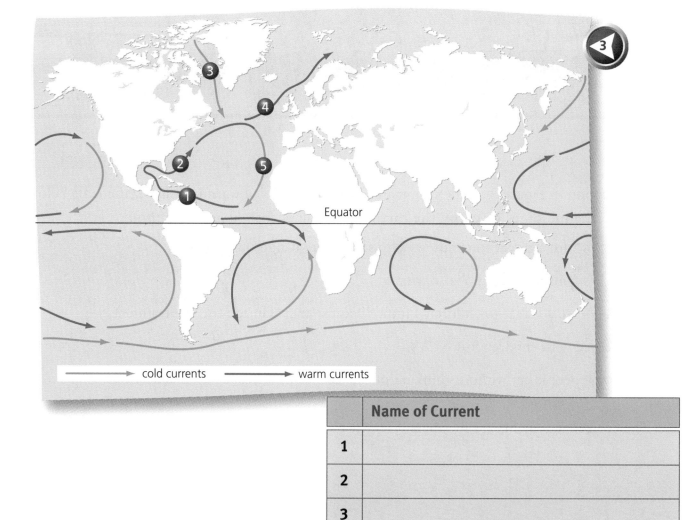

Equator

→ cold currents   → warm currents

	Name of Current
1	
2	
3	
4	
5	

5 Examine Figure 4 and answer the questions that follow.

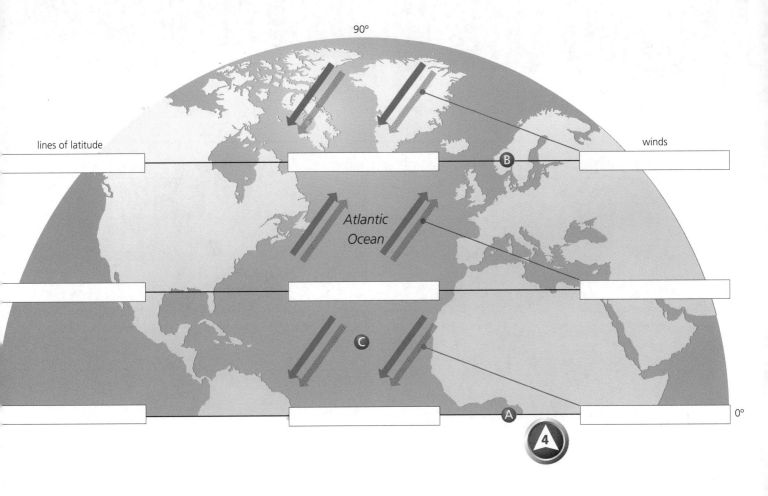

(a) **Circle** the correct response to each of the statements (i) to (v) below:

★ (i) The line of latitude at **A** is called the: *Tropic of Cancer / equator / Tropic of Capricorn*.

★ (ii) When travelling from **A** to **B** on the earth, the climate would:

change from warmer to colder / change from colder to warmer / not change at all.

★ (iii) The winds that blow over Ireland are called the: *Trade Winds / Anti-Trade Winds*.

★ (iv) The area at **A** is known as the: *Doldrums / Horse Latitudes*.

★ (v) The winds at **C** tend to *warm / cool* the areas over which they blow.

(b) Complete Figure 4 by filling in the boxes in the diagram.

(i) *The lines of latitude* (in the boxes on the left side).

(ii) *High pressure or low pressure* (in the boxes in the centre).

(iii) *The names of winds* (in the boxes on the right).

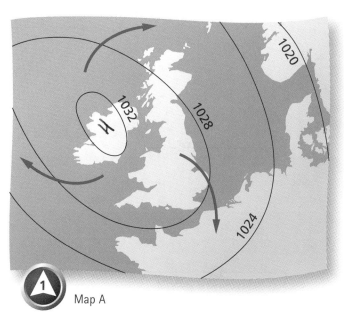

Map A

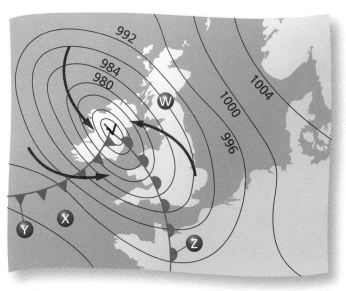

Map B

1 Examine the weather maps A and B in Figure 1 above.

(a) On these maps the numbered lines are called _____.

(b) The numbers on the lines indicate atmospheric pressure measured in _____.

(c) The missing number at **W** on Map B is _____.

(d) The place at **X** (on Map B) is called the _____ sector.

(e) The feature labelled **Y** is a _____.

(f) The feature labelled **Z** is a _____.

(g) The concentrated area of low pressure over Ireland on Map B is called a _____.

(h) On Map B are winds over Ireland strong or gentle? _____

(i) Insert the word 'HIGH' in an appropriate place on Map A.

(j) The most likely weather conditions brought by the air mass shown on Map A are
low / high pressure with *much / little* moisture and *settled / unsettled* weather conditions.
(Circle the correct alternatives.)

2 Contrast the probable weather situations over Ireland, as shown by the two weather maps in Figure 1, under each of the headings given below.

Map A	Barometric pressure	Map B
_____		_____
_____		_____
_____		_____

Winds	
_____	_____
_____	_____
_____	_____

Cloud	
_____	_____
_____	_____
_____	_____

Precipitation	
_____	_____
_____	_____
_____	_____

Fun puzzle

- Solve this spiral word puzzle, which begins at the outside and finishes at the centre.
- The last letter of each solution is also the first letter of the next solution. These letters have already been written in.
- Most of the answers relate to material covered in Chapters 10 and 11.
- Three words have been completed to start you off.

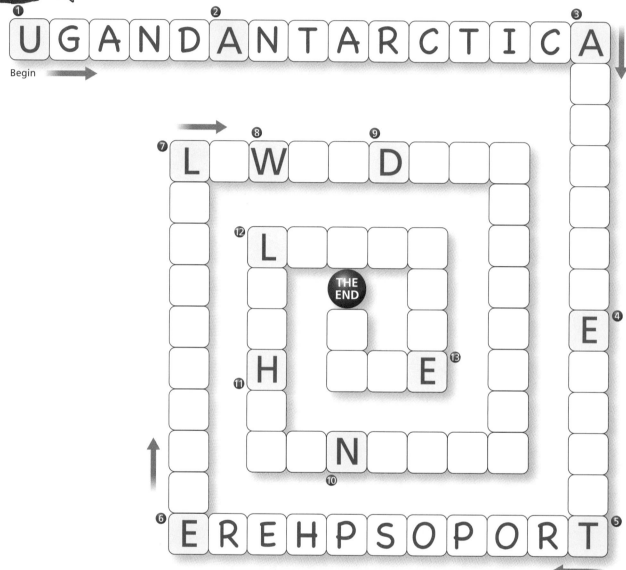

Begin →

Clues

1. An African country near the equator.
2. A very cold landmass near and on the South Pole.
3. Height above sea level.
4. The Greenhouse _ _ _ _ _ _.
5. That part of the atmosphere closest to the earth.
6. The North _ _ _ _ _ _ _ _ Current is at low latitudes.
7. Another word for a depression.
8. Moving air.
9. The spread of deserts.
10. The _ _ _ _ _ Atlantic Drift.
11. A type of precipitation.
12. Angular distance from the equator.
13. Trade winds in the northern hemisphere blow generally from the north _ _ _ _.

Chapter 13

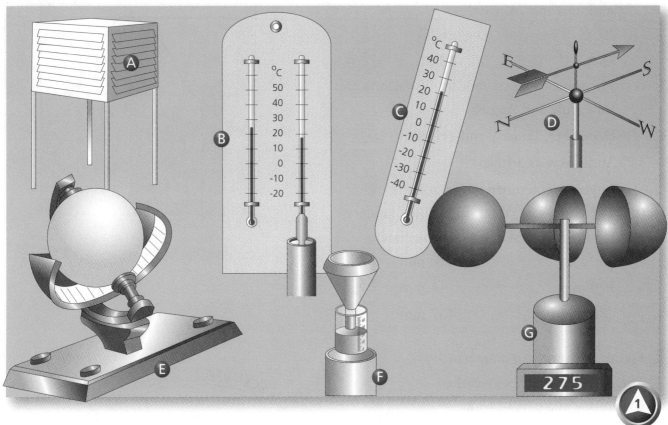

1 Examine Figure 1. In the table below identify the following:

(a) the name of each of the objects or instruments labelled A–G;

(b) what each of the instruments B–G is used to measure;

(c) the unit of measurement related to each of the instruments labelled B–G.

	Object or instrument	What it measures	Unit of measurement
A			
B			
C	Thermometer		
D			
E			Hours per day
F		Precipitation	
G			

2 Examine the weather graph for Valentia, Co. Kerry in Figure 2.
Answer each of the questions (a)–(d) below by ticking the correct boxes.

★ (a) The heaviest rainfall is experienced in:

spring ☐   autumn ☐

summer ☐   winter ☐

★ (b) The average annual temperature at this weather
station is approximately:

29°C ☐   0°C ☐

58°C ☐   10°C ☐

★ (c) The three warmest months in Valentia are:

June, July and August ☐

December, January and February ☐

April, May and June ☐

August, September and October ☐

(d) The combined (total) rainfall for January,
February and March is approximately:

360 mm ☐   120 mm ☐

170 mm ☐   44 mm ☐

35 mm ☐   437 mm ☐

3 Figure 3 shows a *circular weather graph*, which describes weather conditions in a part of India.
Identify each of the following:

(a) the hottest month

_____

(b) the mean temperature of the coolest month

_____

(c) the annual temperature range

_____

(d) the driest month

_____

(e) the approximate amount of rainfall in the wettest month

_____

★ **4** (a) Look at the data below, which shows weather conditions during a seven-day period.

Climate date for Dublin Airport, September 2007

Date	Average Temperature (°C)	Rainfall (mm)	Sunshine (hrs)	Wind direction
1	14.4	0.9	3.7	W
2	12.1	12.6	1.0	S
3	16.8	11.3	1.7	S
4	14.5	10.4	6.3	SW
5	14.7	0.0	4.1	SW
6	13.5	1.6	4.0	SW
7	15.1	0.4	0.0	W

Circle the correct answer in *each* of the following sentences.

(i) The **temperature range** over the seven-day period was *4.7°C / 2.4°C*.

(ii) The **total precipitation** for the week was *38.4 mm / 37.2 mm*.

(iii) The day with the **least** amount of sunshine was *day 2 / day 7*.

(b) Use the data above to complete the wind rose and the sunshine bar graphs in Figures 4 and 5.

Wind rose showing wind direction during a period of seven days at Dublin Airport in September 2007.

▢ Each box represents one day. There are, for example, two boxes on the western (W) branch of the wind rose because wind direction was from the west on two of the seven days given.

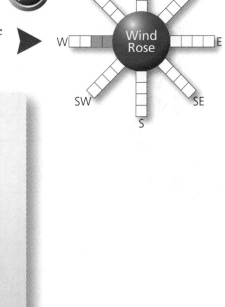

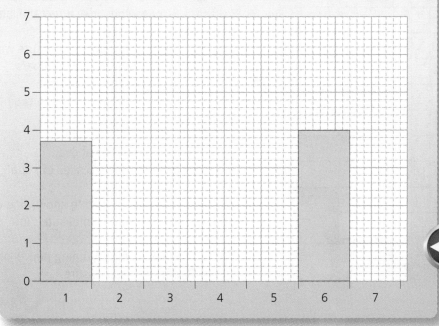

Bar graph showing **hours of sunshine** during a seven-day period at Dublin Airport in September 2007

39

★ **5** Examine the temperature and precipitation statistics for a town in Central Europe.

Month	J	F	M	A	M	J	J	A	S	O	N	D
Temperature (°C)	−4.5	−0.5	2.5	6.0	8.5	12.5	16.0	17.5	12.5	6.5	2.0	−1.0
Precipitation (mm)	11	15	42	36	62	75	99	97	31	32	24	19

Circle the correct answer in *each* of the statements below:

(i) The annual **temperature range** is *22°C / 13°C*.

(ii) The **mean** temperature for the four months from September to December is *5°C / 5.5°C*.

(iii) A *hygrometer / rain gauge* was used to measure rainfall levels to make this chart.

Funtime!

Test your knowledge of Chapter 13 with this bumper word puzzle. You may have to search outside Chapter 13 of your textbook to answer the clues that are **circled**.

Clues Down

1. Instrument used to measure sunshine.

Clues Across

2. Another word for centigrade.
3. Temperature _ _ _ _ _ is the difference between highest and lowest temperatures.
4. Instrument used to measure temperature.
5. Relative humidity is expressed in these.
6. This scale measures wind in 'forces'.
7. White wooden box with louvred sides.
8. Barometric pressure is measured in these.
9. A hygrometer is used to calculate _ _ _ _ _ _ _ _ humidity.
10. Lines on maps joining places of equal wind speeds.
11. Lines on maps joining places of equal temperatures.
12. Another word for a weather chart.
13. Strong winds may affect the landing or _ _ _ _-off of aircraft.
14. Instrument used to measure wind speed.
15. This is measured in millibars.
16. Used to measure rainfall.
17. Lines on maps joining places of equal sunshine.
18. A depression or 'low'.
19. Opposite of 18 above.
20. Isohyets show places of equal _ _ _ _ _ _ _ _.
21. Instrument used to show wind direction.
22. Precipitation is measured in _ _ _ _ _ _ _ _ _ _.
23. Lines on maps joining places of equal barometric pressure.

Test Yourself eTest.ie

1 Complete the passage below by filling in the blank spaces.

Use words from the selection box provided.

Selection Box

- winds
- relief
- Kerry
- rain shadow
- altitude
- prevailing
- precipitation
- concentrated
- West
- leeward
- temperate
- low
- latitude
- sea

Factors which affect climate include _____ or distance from the equator, prevailing _____ and the distance a place is from the _____. Local climates are affected by _____ and _____.

Places in _____ latitudes are usually hotter than places which are far from the equator. This is so because the sun shines more directly and solar energy is therefore more _____ in places near the equator.

The winds that blow most usually are called the _____ winds. In Ireland, these come from the southwest and bring _____ conditions with cool summers and mild winters. They also bring _____ because they absorb moisture over the ocean before they arrive in Ireland.

Aspect can also affect the precipitation levels of local climates. Places on the windward sides of coastal mountains may get relief rainfall, while places on the _____ sides of mountains may be dry, _____ areas. The mountains of _____ and of Connemara in the _____ of Ireland are thus affected by aspect.

2 *Circle* the correct alternative in each statement below.

(a) The prevailing wind in the West of Ireland is *on shore / off shore*.

(b) Ireland has a *large / small* annual temperature range.

(c) Northerly air masses bring *dry / wet* weather conditions to Ireland.

(d) Southerly slopes of European mountains receive more *direct / slanted* sunrays than northerly slopes. This causes northerly slopes to be *warmer / colder* than southerly slopes.

(e) Air temperatures are *lower / higher* at the foot of a mountain than at the summit.

★ **3** Which of the following statements **best** describes Ireland's climate?

Very cold winters, short summers with light rain ☐

Hot and dry summers, cold and dry winters ☐

Mild winters, warm summers, rainfall throughout the year ☐

Tick (✓) the correct box.

4 *'Altitude and aspect can each affect the local climate of an area.'*
Examine the diagram below and answer the questions that follow.

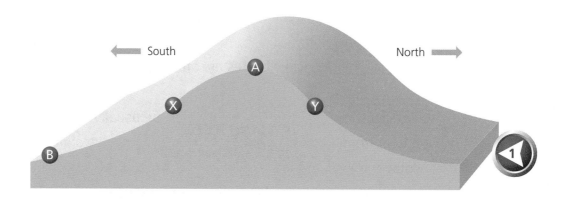

★ (a) Explain *one reason* why the place labelled **A** is likely to be colder than the place labelled **B**.

_____

_____

_____

_____

★ (b) Explain *one reason* why the place labelled **X** is likely to be warmer than the place labelled **Y**.

_____

_____

_____

_____

5 Study the climate figures for Valentia (West Kerry) in the table below.

Month	J	F	M	A	M	J	J	A	S	O	N	D
Temperature (°C)	5	7	8	11	13	14	15	15	14	12	8	6
Precipitation (mm)	122	95	80	59	45	35	15	18	40	74	122	142

(a) Which month has the lowest average temperature in Valentia? _____

(b) What is the highest monthly temperature in Valentia? _____

(c) What is the annual *temperature range* in Valentia? _____

(d) What is the mean monthly temperature for November, December, January and February *combined*? _____

(e) What is the total annual rainfall? _____

Funtime!

Clues

1. Southerly winds over Ireland are _____ because they come from lower latitudes.
2. This Eastern European capital city has very cold winters.
3. Climate is average _____ over a long period.
4. South-westerly winds might bring this to Ireland.
5. A factor affecting climate.
6. This line of latitude is at the lowest latitude.
7. A factor that affects local climates.
8. This northern EU country has a generally cold climate.
9. A low pressure belt at the equator.
10. Winds from this direction are usually warm and may bring rain to Ireland.
11. Ireland's summers are not as _____ as those in Mediterranean countries.
12. Ireland's climate is _____ It does not have extremes of temperature.
13. A North African country with a hot desert climate.
14. An instrument used to measure temperatures.
15. This type of rainfall may be common on the seaward slopes of mountains.

Begin this wheel puzzle on the outside by finding the word referred to in clue 1. Then follow the clues to work inwards to the end. The last letter of each hidden word is also the first letter of the next word. Each of these last/first letters is included to help you. The first and second words are also completed to start you off.

1 Link each of the terms in Column X with its pair in Column Y. One match has been made already.

Column X			Column Y	
1	Atacama	A	Prevail over hot desert areas	
2	Tap roots	B	Not planted by people	
3	Cereus	C	A hot desert in South America	
4	Mesquite	D	A night-blooming plant	
5	Trade winds	E	A desert place made fertile by water	
6	Oasis	F	A deep-rooted desert plant	
7	Natural vegetation	G	Absorb deep water underground	

1	
2	
3	
4	
5	
6	E
7	

2 Study the map in Figure 1 and circle the correct answers in each case.

⭐ (a) The climatic type found at A is *hot desert / tundra*.

The climatic type found at B is *equatorial / temperate*.

The climatic type found at C is *boreal / savanna*.

The climatic type found at D is *equatorial / savanna*.

(b) In the spaces provided, name the hot deserts labelled E, F, G and H on the map.

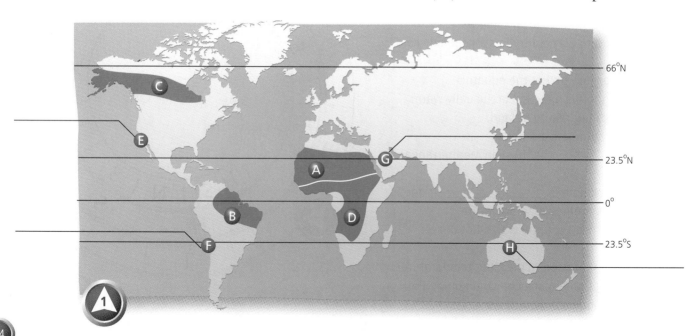

3 The data in Figure 2 gives temperature and rainfall figures for the town of Bilma in Niger, Africa.

BILMA	J	F	M	A	M	J	J	A	S	O	N	D
Temperature (°C)	17	20	25	29	32	33	33	33	32	28	23	19
Rain (mm)	0	0	0	0	1	1	2	9	4	2	0	0

(a) Use the data in Figure 2 to construct in Figure 3 a set of bar graphs to illustrate the monthly precipitation figures for Bilma. One bar has been made for you.

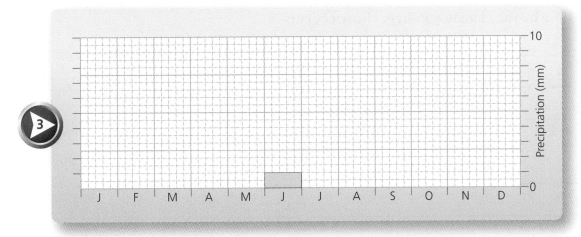

(b) Use the data in Figure 2 to complete the following passage by circling the correct *alternatives*.

The town of Bilma experiences a *Mediterranean / desert* type climate. It is *very hot / warm* in winter and *very hot / warm* in summer. The hottest months are from *May / June* to August, when temperatures average *32° / 33°* degrees Celsius. The coolest month is *December / January*, with a temperature of *17 / 19* degrees. The annual range of temperature is *16 / 18* degrees.

The climate here is *extremely / fairly* dry. No rain is recorded for the *five / six* months from November to *March / April*. The total annual rainfall is a mere *19 / 21* millimetres.

(c) *Account for* the fact that the climate of places such as Bilma are:

Hot: _____

_____

_____

Dry: _____

_____

_____

★ **4** Choose **one** type of climate you have studied.

(a) Describe what the climate is like – refer to temperature and rainfall.

Temperature: _____

_____

Rainfall: _____

_____

(b) Explain why the climate you have chosen occurs.

_____

_____

_____

_____

_____

_____

5 **Word Puzzle**

The map in Figure 4 shows countries of the Sahara desert. Use your atlas to find the names of these countries and use them to solve the word puzzle. The country labelled '1a' on the map is the '1 across' clue on the puzzle. The country labelled '2d' is the '2 down' clue and so on.

Chapter 17

1 Select the statements given in the box to *complete the diagram* in Figure 1.

How rapid population growth can help cause deforestation

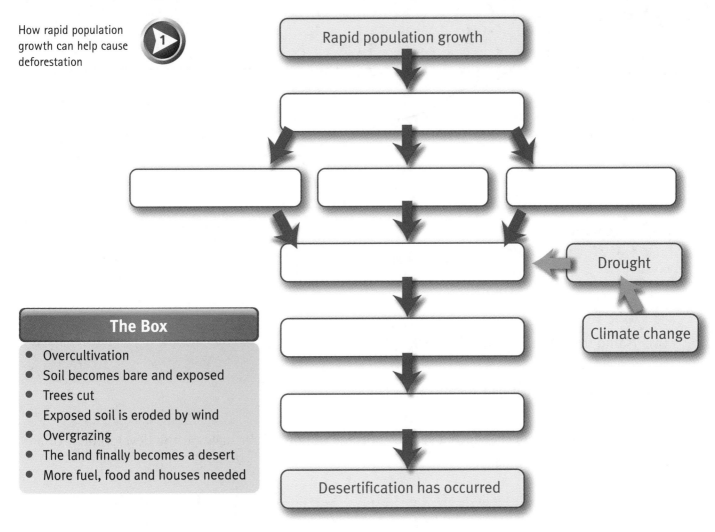

The Box

- Overcultivation
- Soil becomes bare and exposed
- Trees cut
- Exposed soil is eroded by wind
- Overgrazing
- The land finally becomes a desert
- More fuel, food and houses needed

Rapid population growth

Drought

Climate change

Desertification has occurred

★ 2 In the boxes provided, match each letter in Column X with the number of its pair in Column Y. One pair has been completed.

	Column X
A	Moving water
B	Severe drought occurred here
C	Low atmospheric pressure
D	High pressure system
E	Sulphur dioxide

	Column Y
1	Acid rain
2	Ascending air
3	Ocean current
4	Dry weather conditions
5	The Sahel

A	
B	5
C	
D	
E	

3 The graph shows how rainfall levels changed over time in Somalia between 1960 and 2006.

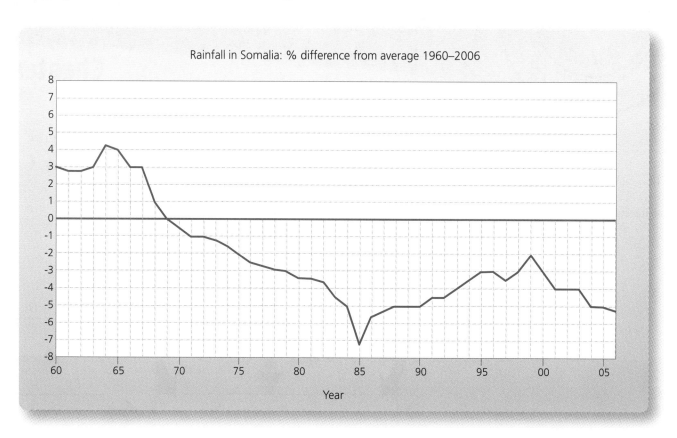

(a) Name the year that had the least rainfall. _____

(b) Name the year that had the most rainfall. _____

(c) Describe **three** effects which a severe shortage of rain might have on the development of a country such as Somalia.

1 _____

_____

2 _____

_____

3 _____

_____

Chapter 18

1 With the aid of the map in Figure 1 and your knowledge of irrigation schemes, fill in the gaps and circle the correct *alternatives* in the passage given here.

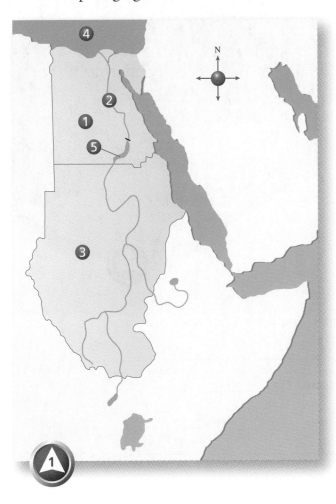

1

Most of E_____ (labelled 1 on the map) is part of the S_____ desert. But the *western / eastern* part of the country is drained by the River N_____ (2 on map). This river flows through S_____ (3 on map) before flowing *northwards / southwards* through Egypt. It meets the _____ Sea (4 on map), by means of a large *estuary / delta*.

In times past, the river Nile flooded for *all / part* of the year, but did not provide enough water to *drain / irrigate* the land at other times. The Aswan Dam was built during the *1960s / 1990s* to control flooding, to provide water for irrigation and to generate *thermal / hydroelectric* power. Lake _____ (5 on map) also provides facilities for *fish / organic* farming and helps to provide domestic water supplies for *thousands / millions* of Egyptians.

But the Aswan project has also created problems. When the Nile flooded annually, it *deposited / eroded* valuable *marine / alluvial* mud, which was useful to the *farmers / fisherpeople*. This mud is no longer available. The formation of Lake Nasser on the *upstream / downstream* side of the dam flooded people's homes, as well as the sites of ancient *churches / tombs*. *High / low* temperatures also caused *condensation / evaporation* on the surface of the lake. This led to a *loss / increase* of salt in the water, which can *improve / damage* the land being irrigated.

2 In the boxes provided, match each letter in Column X with the number of its pair in Column Y.

	Column X
1	Unusually long rainless period
2	Artificial watering of land
3	Build-up of salt in water
4	Soil or mud deposited by rivers

	Column Y
A	Alluvium
B	Salinisation
C	Drought
D	Irrigation

X	Y
A	
B	
C	
D	

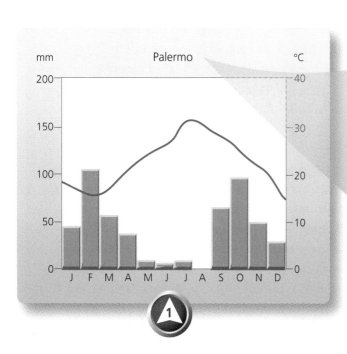

1 Figure 1 shows precipitation bars and a temperature graph for Palermo.

   (a) In which *island* and *country* is Palermo? _____ _____

   (b) Name the type of climate that is shaded in Figure 1(a). _____

   (c) Identify each of the following from Figure 1:

   - The hottest month and its temperature _____ _____

   - The approximate annual temperature range _____

   - The wettest month and its precipitation _____ _____

   - The driest month and its precipitation _____ _____

   - Account for temperature levels in Palermo throughout the year.

   _____

   _____

   _____

Important!

Junior Certificate Marking Schemes and Model Answers

A Hints on answering Junior Certificate questions

1 **Read each question very carefully** so that you understand exactly what the question is asking. Take care that your answer remains on the point of the question. Remember that **no** marks will be awarded for off-the-point information.

2 If a question asks you to **name** or to **identify** something, name or identify the object as precisely as possible. Merely name the object. There are **no** extra marks for describing it.

- **Sample question**: *Name one Mediterranean region in the Southern Hemisphere.*
- **Full-mark answer**: Central Chile. ✓

3 If you are asked to **describe**, **explain** or otherwise **expand** on something, you must **develop your answer**. A developed answer should include *a statement and up to three development points* of information at Higher Level. A statement and one or two development points will suffice at Ordinary Level. Each point of information can be short and simple, provided it is relevant. Points may include **examples** or refer to reasons for something.

- **Sample question**: *Explain how the natural vegetation of Mediterranean lands is suited to the Mediterranean climate.*
- **Full-mark answer**: *Some trees have small waxy leaves.* ✓ *The olive tree is an example.* ✓ *Such trees do not lose moisture through transpiration.* ✓ *Transpiration is the loss of moisture through the bark.* ✓

4 In all examinations, **manage your time carefully** so that you answer all the questions required of you as perfectly as you can.

5 **Have confidence**. Most Junior Certificate questions are straightforward, so do not look for 'hidden tricks' in them. If you study your textbook well, you will cover the entire Junior Certificate course and are likely to find almost all questions quite easy.

It is important to understand how Junior Certificate examination questions are marked and to be aware of what must be written in order to obtain full marks for an answer. Given here are:
(a) some general hints on how to answer questions well;
(b) some sample Junior Certificate questions with marking schemes;
(c) a sample 'full-mark' answer to a Junior Certificate question.

B Sample Junior Certificate examination question

The Mediterranean area has hot, dry summers and mild, moist winters.

Q Explain why weather conditions are so different in summer and in winter in Mediterranean areas. *(10 marks)*
(J.C. Higher Level, 2000)

Marking Scheme

This question asks for **reasons for** the main features of Mediterranean climate in **summer** and in **winter**.

The 10 marks set aside for the question include *5 marks* for development explanation(s) of **summer** conditions and *5 marks* for development explanation(s) of **winter** conditions.

Each *5 marks* is awarded as follows:
Statement = *2 marks*
First development = *1 mark*
Second development = *1 mark*
Third development = *1 mark*

To ensure full marks always try to write one **extra development**.

C Full-Mark Answer

Summers are hot and dry because:

- The area is less than 40 degrees from the equator. ✓ (2 marks)
- Therefore the sun is high in the sky and gives great heat. ✓ (1 mark)
- High pressure dominates the area in summer. ✓ (1 mark)
- This brings dry, settled weather. ✓ (1 mark)

Winters are mild and moist because:

- Even in winter, the sun is high enough in the sky to give quite warm conditions. ✓ (2 marks)
- Prevailing winds blow in from the Atlantic. ✓ (1 mark)
- These winds carry depressions. ✓ (1 mark)
- Depressions bring wet, unsettled conditions. ✓ (1 mark)

Now answer the two Junior Certificate questions on page 53 and correct them using the marking schemes indicated.

2 Study the diagram below.

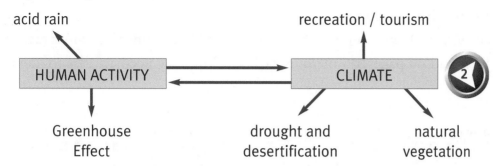

Write two sentences to describe what the diagram shows. *(6 marks)*

(a) _____

_____

_____

(b) _____

_____

_____

> **Marking Scheme**
> Two sentences at *3 marks* each.
> Each sentence should refer to at least two linkages (connections) given in the diagram.

3 *The tourist industry of many countries depends on climate.*

Explain how (a) a warm climate and (b) a cold climate can help to attract tourists to a country. Name a country in each case. *(12 marks)*

(a) _____

_____

_____

_____

_____

_____

(b) _____

_____

_____

_____

_____

_____

> **Marking Scheme**
> How a warm climate attracts tourists = 6 marks
> How a cold climate attracts tourists = 6 marks
> Each 6 marks is *awarded as follows*:
> Statement = *2 marks*
> First development = *1 mark*
> Second development = *1 mark*
> A country named = *2 marks*

> **Reminder:**
> Try to include *one extra development* in each explanation.

New Complete Geography Workbook

Word Puzzle
Mediterranean and mountain tourism

Use the clues on the map (Figure 3) to complete the word puzzle. The countries, tourist regions and cities in the puzzle can be found on page 106 of your textbook. You may need an atlas to identify the mountains.

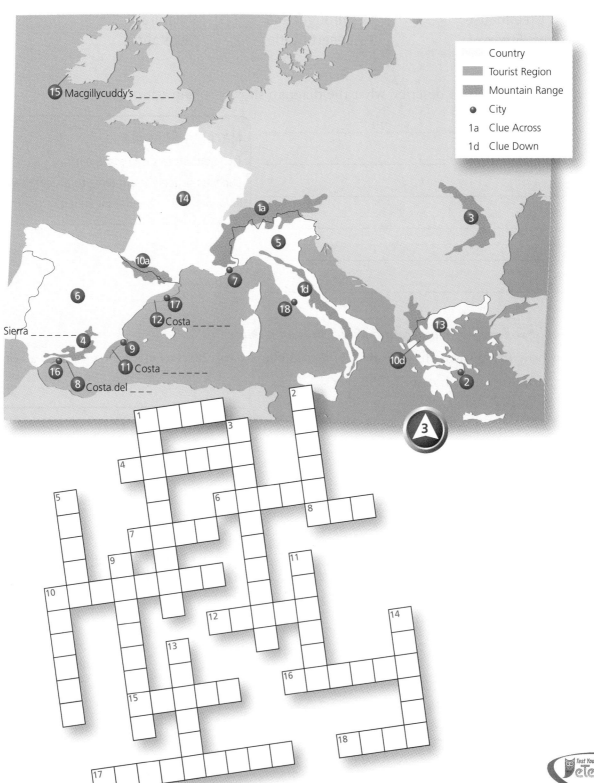

Chapter 20

1 Study the map and *circle* the correct answer in each of the sentences below.

★ (a) The climate type found at A is *hot desert / tundra*.

(b) The climate type found at B is *equatorial / temperate oceanic*.

(c) The climate type found at C is *savanna / boreal*.

(d) A country with boreal climate is *Sweden / Brazil*.

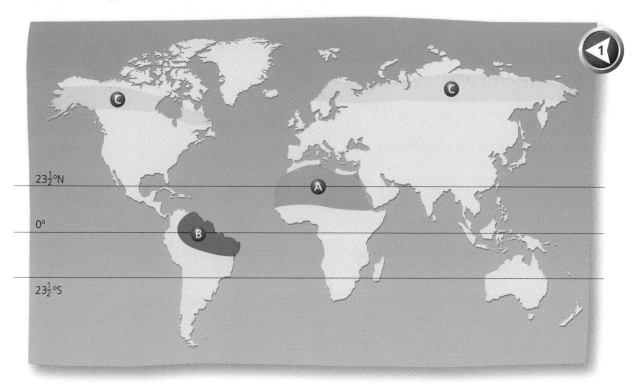

2 With reference to Figure 2 explain briefly how each of the features labelled **A–C** helps to make coniferous trees suited to the climate of boreal lands.

A _____

_____

B _____

_____

C _____

_____

3 Look at the climate figures in Figure 3.

(a) Which of the following climate types is most likely to be shown by the figures?

savanna type ☐

tundra type ☐

warm temperate oceanic type ☐

cool temperate oceanic type ☐

(b) The *maximum monthly temperature* is

_____.

(c) The *coldest* month is _____.

Month	Mean temp (°C)	Mean precip. (mm)
January	−26	5.0
February	−28	2.5
March	−26	2.5
April	−18	2.5
May	−8	2.5
June	1	7.5
July	4	23.0
August	4	20.0
September	−1	13.0
October	−8	13.0
November	−17	7.5
December	−24	5.0

(d) Which of the following is the correct *annual temperature range* for this weather station?

32°C ☐   12°C ☐   −24°C ☐   −12°C ☐

(e) The *minimum monthly temperature* is _____.

(f) The *wettest month* is _____.

(g) Which of the following is the correct total annual precipitation figure for this weather station?

23mm ☐   94mm ☐   104mm ☐   20.5mm ☐

4 Use the statistics in Figure 3 to complete the precipitation graph in Figure 4.

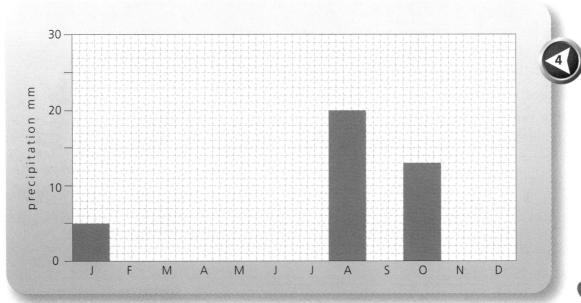

Chapter 21

1 Indicate whether each of the following statements is true or false (circle the *True* or *False* alternative in each case).

(a) Relatively little natural vegetation exists in Western Europe.   *True / False*

(b) Hot, wet regions of the world tend to have thick forests.   *True / False*

(c) As temperatures increase, vegetation usually becomes more scarce.   *True / False*

(d) Most types of vegetation will not grow below 4°C.   *True / False*

In the boxes provided in Figure 1, explain how climate affects natural vegetation.

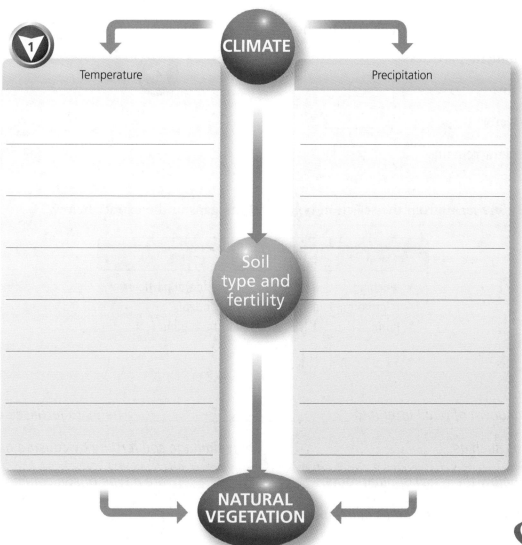

★ **1** The divided bar chart shows the composition of soil.

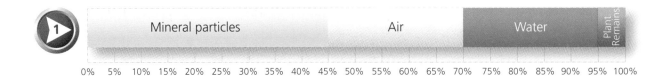

| Mineral particles | Air | Water | Plant Remains |

0% 5% 10% 15% 20% 25% 30% 35% 40% 45% 50% 55% 60% 65% 70% 75% 80% 85% 90% 95% 100%

(a) Label the pie chart in Figure 2, using the information on the divided bar in Figure 1.

(b) What percentage of the bar chart shows:

- mineral particles   _____

- air   _____

- water   _____

- plant remains   _____

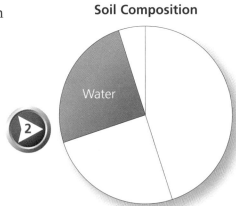

Soil Composition

Water

★ **2** Choose *three terms* from the selection box to fill the gaps in the extract below.

Selection Box

- leaching
- micro-organisms
- humus
- mineral particles
- podzols
- hard pans

The breakdown of plant litter into _____ helps to fertilise soil.

Processes such as _____ may damage soil fertility by causing nutrients

to seep below the reach of plant roots. _____ are a type of soil commonly

found in damp highland areas in Ireland.

3 How soil is formed

Use the words in the selection box to fill in the blank spaces in Figure 3.

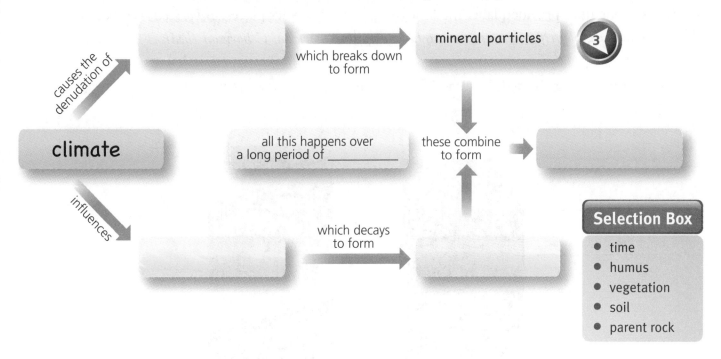

causes the denudation of

which breaks down to form

mineral particles

3

climate

all this happens over a long period of _____

these combine to form

influences

which decays to form

Selection Box
- time
- humus
- vegetation
- soil
- parent rock

4 Study the map of Ireland's principal soil types in Figure 4.

★ (a) What is the most common soil type in Ireland?

_____

★ (b) What is the most common soil type in the South East of Ireland?

_____

★ (c) What is the most common soil type in the upland areas of the North West?

_____

(d) What is the most common soil type in each of the following counties?

- Co. Dublin _____
- Co. Donegal _____
- Co. Derry _____

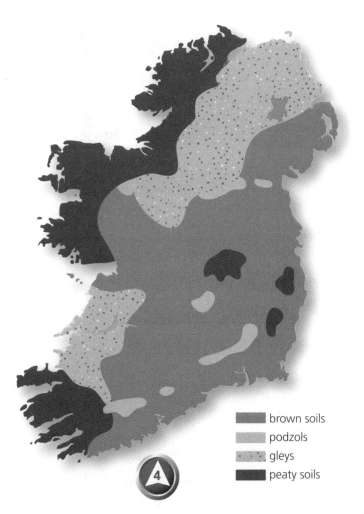

4

- brown soils
- podzols
- gleys
- peaty soils

5 Figures 5 and 6 show contrasting soil profiles. One shows the profile of podzols and the other of brown soils.

(a) On the lines provided label the following in their correct places: *B-horizon; brown A-horizon; hardpan; plentiful humus near surface; greyish A-horizon; C-horizon (bedrock); leaching; plant litter*

(b) In the boxes provided, label *podzol profile* and *brown soils profile*.

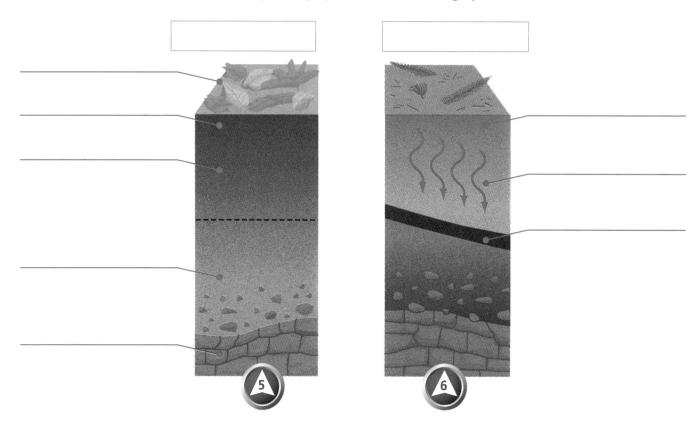

★ 6 Choose two Irish soil types and describe any three differences between them.

Soil type 1: _____   Soil type 2: _____

Differences:

1 _____

_____

2 _____

_____

3 _____

_____

Test yourself . . .
. . . with this Junior Cert Higher Level question. Use the official marking scheme and sample answers to help you.

★ **7** (i) Explain two ways in which soil is important to humans. *(4 marks)*

Starter sample answer:
Soils are needed to grow farm crops, 1 ✓
which provide us with the food we need 1 ✓

Official Marking Scheme

(i) *Two explanations get 2 marks each. In each explanation give 1 mark for a statement and 1 mark for a development.*

Reminder:
Try to write *one* **extra development** in each explanation.

Now explain two other ways:

1 _____

_____

2 _____

_____

(ii) With reference to *two* of the following factors, explain their role in soil formation:

- original rock
- climate
- micro-organisms
- vegetation *(6 marks)*

Official Marking Scheme

(ii) *Two explanations get 3 marks each. In each explanation give 2 marks for a statement and 1 mark for a development.*

Starter sample answer:
The original rock is weathered and eroded by frost, water, etc 2 ✓
It breaks down into small mineral particles, which make up part of the soil. 1 ✓

Now write about two other factors:

1 _____

_____

2 _____

_____

Field Studies

8 Comparing Two Soil Samples

A local study which can be carried out in class.

Equipment needed

- two large jars
- several strips of universal indicator paper (ask a science teacher for some)
- some distilled water
- hand magnifying glasses (if available)

Method

- Fill two large jars with soil samples. Take one sample from a deciduous woodland and the other from a coniferous woodland.
- Divide the class into several teams of four. Give each team separate soil samples, one from each of the two jars.
- The teams should carry out their soil sample tests as outlined below.
- Each student should use the table in Figure 8 to record his or her findings.

Tests

A. *Plant litter and humus*

- Examine the type of plant litter and the amount of humus contained in each soil sample. If necessary, use a hand magnifying glass.

B. *Colour*

- Describe carefully the colour of each soil sample.

C. *Acid/alkaline test*

- Test the acidity/alkalinity of each soil sample. Use the method described in Figure 7 and at the top of page 63.

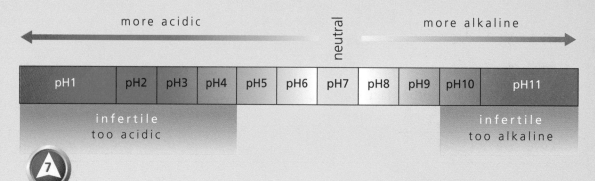

The pH indicator shows whether the soil is acidic or alkaline

Dampen some soil with a little distilled water. Then press a piece of clean universal indicator paper against the soil. The change in the paper's colour will show the pH value of the soil.
(See indicator key in the indicator paper pack.) The pH value indicates whether the soil is acidic or alkaline in nature. Figure 7 indicates that neutral soils are more fertile than soils which are either very acidic or very alkaline.

Soil sample from a deciduous woodland located at

_____

_____

A. Type of plant litter _____

Humus content:

_____ a lot

_____ some

_____ none

B. Colour of soil _____

C. Acid/alkaline:

_____ acidic

_____ slightly acid

_____ neutral

_____ slightly alkaline

_____ alkaline

Soil sample from a deciduous woodland located at

_____

_____

A. Type of plant litter _____

Humus content:

_____ a lot

_____ some

_____ none

B. Colour of soil _____

C. Acid/alkaline:

_____ acidic

_____ slightly acid

_____ neutral

_____ slightly alkaline

_____ alkaline

Conclusions and contrasts

Record any contrasts you have observed between the two soil samples. Say which of the soil samples you consider to be more fertile. Give a reason/reasons for your answer.

_____

_____

_____

_____

_____

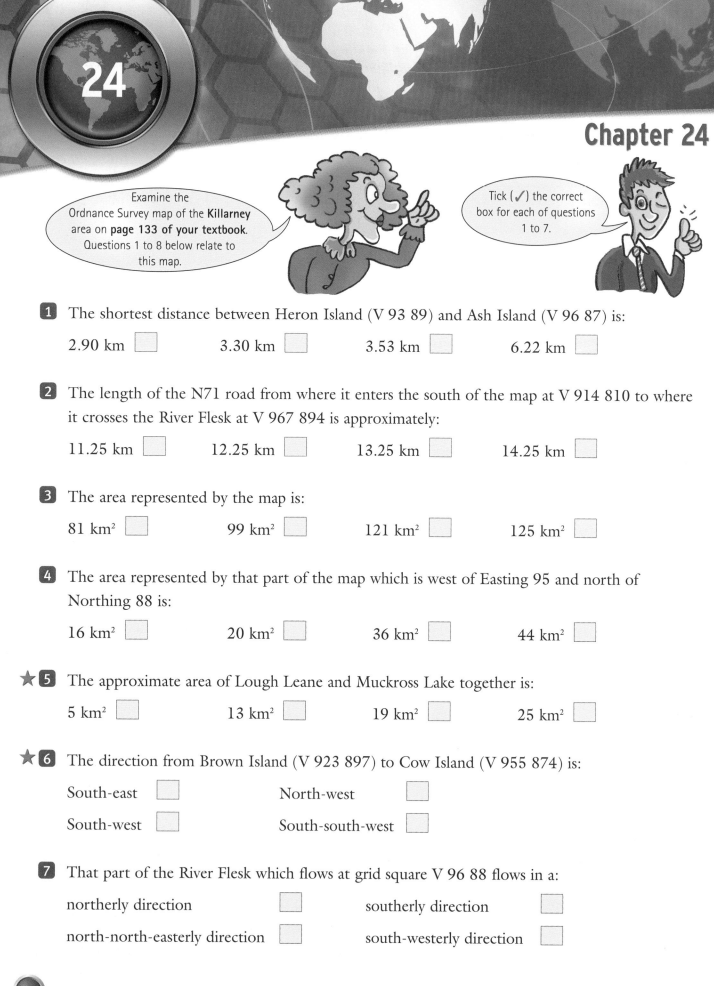

Examine the Ordnance Survey map of the **Killarney** area on **page 133 of your textbook**. Questions 1 to 8 below relate to this map.

Tick (✓) the correct box for each of questions 1 to 7.

1 The shortest distance between Heron Island (V 93 89) and Ash Island (V 96 87) is:

2.90 km ☐   3.30 km ☐   3.53 km ☐   6.22 km ☐

2 The length of the N71 road from where it enters the south of the map at V 914 810 to where it crosses the River Flesk at V 967 894 is approximately:

11.25 km ☐   12.25 km ☐   13.25 km ☐   14.25 km ☐

3 The area represented by the map is:

81 km² ☐   99 km² ☐   121 km² ☐   125 km² ☐

4 The area represented by that part of the map which is west of Easting 95 and north of Northing 88 is:

16 km² ☐   20 km² ☐   36 km² ☐   44 km² ☐

★5 The approximate area of Lough Leane and Muckross Lake together is:

5 km² ☐   13 km² ☐   19 km² ☐   25 km² ☐

★6 The direction from Brown Island (V 923 897) to Cow Island (V 955 874) is:

South-east ☐   North-west ☐

South-west ☐   South-south-west ☐

7 That part of the River Flesk which flows at grid square V 96 88 flows in a:

northerly direction ☐   southerly direction ☐

north-north-easterly direction ☐   south-westerly direction ☐

8 In the boxes provided, match each of the grid references **A–E** in Column X with the number of its pair in Column Y. (These grid references and features relate to the Killarney area OS map.)

Column X	
A	V 928 916
B	V 984 886
C	V 964 858
D	V 971 882
E	V 999 870

Column Y	
A	Boating activities
B	Nature reserve
C	Third-class road
D	Castle
E	Golf course

X	Y
A	
B	
C	
D	
E	

9 (a) Figures **A–D** below show **cross sections** or *side views* of different types of slopes.

- Contours in the map fragments **1-4** represent the slopes shown in A–D, but 1–4 are not given in the same order as A–D.
- In the boxes provided, match each of the numbers 1–4 with the letter of its pair.

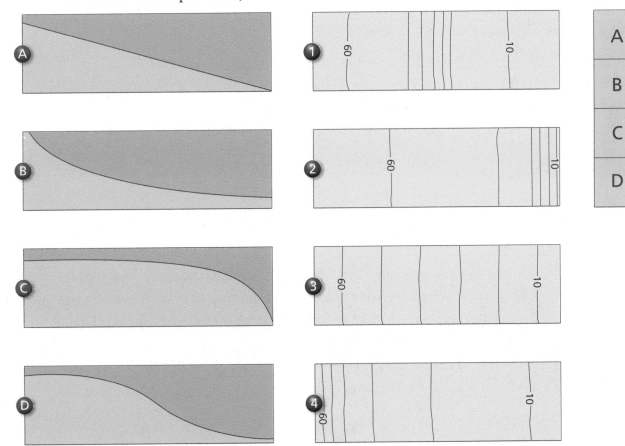

(b) Name the type of slope shown in diagram C. _____

Full Junior Certificate Question, Marking Scheme and Model Answer

On pages 68 and 69 you will find the *OS map* and the *aerial photograph* of the *Ardee area* which appeared in a Junior Certificate examination. Below are Higher Level Junior Certificate questions, marking schemes and sample 'full-mark' answers relating to that map and photograph. Examine the map, photograph and information given below. This will help you to understand what you have to do to obtain full marks in your examination answers.

The Questions

1 Study the Ordnance Survey map of the Ardee area.

   (a)   What is the distance in kilometres along the N2 roadway from the junction with the third class road (N 994 848) to the junction with the R170 road (N 963 903)? *(4 marks)*

   (b)   If you were travelling in a straight line **to** Ardee **from** the following places, in which direction would you be travelling in each case?

      (i)   Philibenstown (O 0094)

      (ii)   Blakestown Cross Roads (N 965 878)

      (iii)   Knocklore (N 931 953) *(6 marks)*

2 Using evidence from the map only, give **three** reasons why Ardee developed at this location. In your answer refer to both the past and the present. *(12 marks)*

3 *(You will be able to answer this question only if you have studied aerial photographs as well as OS maps.)*

   (a)   Using both the photograph and the map of Ardee, state the direction in which the camera was pointing when the photograph was taken. The crossroads at the centre middleground of the photograph is shown at N 962 906 on the OS map. *(2 marks)*

   (b)   At what time of the year was the photograph taken? Suggest two pieces of evidence from the photograph to support your answer. *(6 marks)*

Remember that the answers given to questions 2 and 3 (b) below are only **samples** of information that could be used to obtain full marks. In these cases, other relevant points of information could also be used.

The Marking Scheme	Full-Mark Answers
1 (a) Award *4 marks* for any answer within a range of 7.0 km to 7.5 km only.	**1** (a) 7.3 km
(b) Award 2 marks each for these three directions only: (i) South-west (ii) North (iii) South-east	(b) (i) South-west (ii) North (iii) South-east
2 Award *4 marks* for each of three reasons. At least one reason must refer to the **present** and at least one reason must refer to the **past**. *Allocate each 4 marks as follows:* Statement = 2 marks Development = 1 mark Map evidence = 1 mark **Reminder:** Try to write *one* extra development	**2** (a) Ardee was once a defence point. There are castles to be found, for example at N 962 905. (b) It is a meeting point of roads, for example the N2 and N52. Where roads meet trade develops and settlements grow. (c) It is a bridging point on the River Dee at N 963 904. Roads meet to cross the bridge.
3 (a) Award *2 marks* for the correct direction, which is **north-east**. (b) ● Award *2 marks* for stating the correct time of year. ● Accept any one or combination of the following answers: Summer / May / June / July / August ● Award *2 marks each for two pieces of evidence*. Allocate each of these 2 marks as follows: Statement = 1 mark Evidence from photograph = 1 mark	**3** (a) The direction is north-east. (b) ● The time is summer. (c) ● The crops in the fields are golden or brown, for example in the centre background. Deciduous trees have all their leaves, for example in the left foreground.

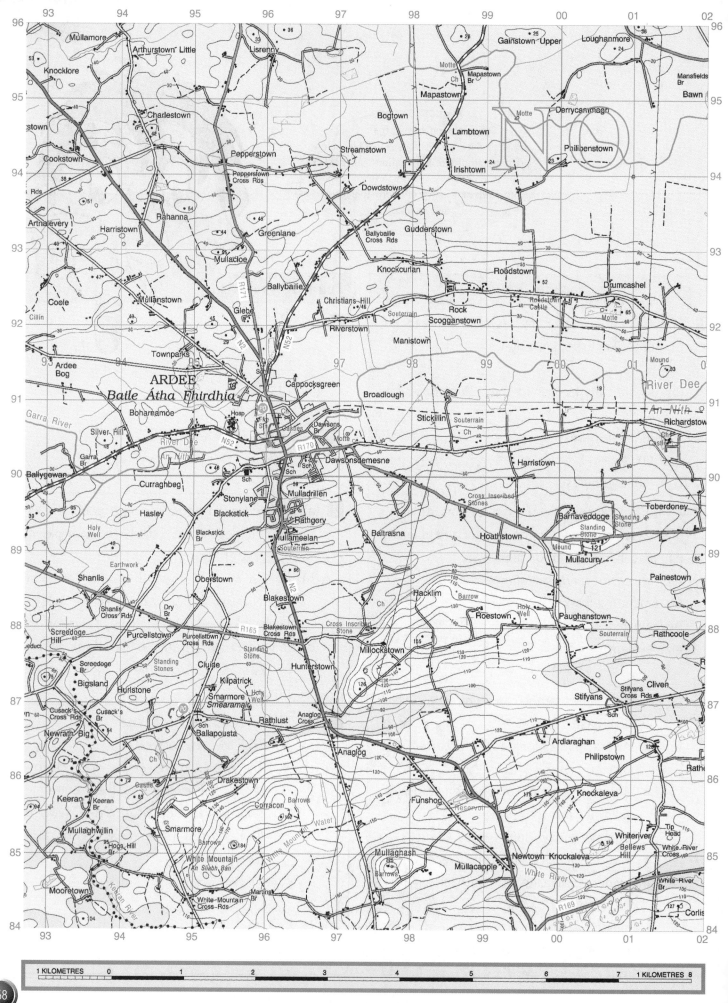

Ardee, Co. Louth *(taken from a Junior Certificate exam paper)*

For You to Do – a Full Junior Certificate Ordnance Survey Map Question (with Marking Scheme)

On pages 66 and 67 you examined Junior Certificate marking schemes and full-mark answers.

On page 148 of your textbook you will find the *OS map* of the *Sligo/Rosses Point* area used in a Junior Certificate examination. Use this map to answer the Junior Certificate Higher Level questions given below. Try to achieve full-mark answers with the help of the marking schemes provided.

Marking Scheme
A. Two different kinds of tourist attraction, one in Drumcliff and one in Rosses Point, will get *4 marks* each. (Note that each tourist attraction must be apparent on the map.) *Allocate each 4 marks as follows:*
Tourist attraction named = *2 marks*
Development/description = *1 mark*
Grid reference location on map = *1 mark*

Reminder: Try to write *one* **extra development** in each explanation or description.

A. The areas around Drumcliff (G 67 42) and Rosses Point (G 63 40) attract tourists for different reasons. Using Ordnance Survey map evidence **only**, describe one type of attraction provided by Rosses Point and a different type of tourist attraction in Drumcliff. (*8 marks*)

Answer: _____

_____

_____

_____

B. (i) What is the distance, in kilometres, along the N15 road from its junction with the R291 (G 69 36) to Drumcliff Bridge (G 67 42)? (*4 marks*)

(ii) Would a climb of *Kings Mountain* (G 703 442) *from the south-east* be steeper than a climb of *Knocknarea* (G 626 346) *from the east*? Explain briefly how you know. (*6 marks*)

Answer (i): _____

_____

_____

Answer (ii): _____

_____

_____

Marking Scheme
B. (i) *Four marks* for correct or near correct answer.
(ii) Allow *2 marks* for identifying the less steep slope.
Allow *4 marks* for 'how you know'.
Allocate these marks as follows:
Statement = *2 marks*
Development or map (grid) reference = *2 marks*

C. The processes of **erosion** and **deposition** have influenced the area shown on the map.

With reference to **two** specific features explain this statement.

Use map evidence to support your answer. (*12 marks*)

Answer: _____

_____

_____

_____

_____

_____

_____

_____

_____

Marking Scheme

C. *Six marks* each should be allocated for a specific feature of erosion and a specific feature of deposition.

Allocate each 6 marks as follows:
Feature identified = 2 marks
Grid reference location of feature = 2 marks
Development/description = 2 marks

Another question relating to the Sligo/Rosses Point map *(See page 148 of your textbook.)*

Use the box provided to draw a **sketch map** of the Sligo/Rosses Point OS map. On your sketch show and name the following:

- the coast
- a national primary road
- two regional roads
- a railway line and railway station
- the built-up area of Sligo town
- Drumcliff River
- a feature of sea deposition

Shade in all land that is higher than 200 metres above sea level.

Give your sketch map a title and insert a North arrow near it.

Full Junior Certificate Aerial Photograph Question, Marking Scheme and Model Answer

On pages 68 and 69 you will find the OS map and the aerial photograph of the *Ardee area* that appeared in a Junior Certificate examination. Below is the Higher Level Junior Certificate aerial photograph question from that examination, together with its marking scheme and sample 'full-mark' answers. Examine these. They will help you to understand what you have to do to obtain full marks in your examination answers.

The Questions	The Marking Scheme
1 Using the photograph only, draw a sketch map of the part of Ardee town shown. On the map mark and identify the following places: (a) two connecting roads; (b) a church and graveyard; (c) a historic building; (d) grain silos; (e) a timber storage area. *(10 marks)*	**1** Award 2 marks for *locating **and** naming* each of the five features demanded. Deduct 1 mark if the sketch map is not correctly framed.
2 (a) *The main street in Ardee runs across the photograph from left middleground to right middleground.* With reference to the photograph, give two pieces of evidence to support the statement that this is Ardee's main street. *(4 marks)* (b) Briefly explain **one** advantage and **one** disadvantage in living along the main street of a town like Ardee. *(6 marks)*	**2** (a) Award *2 marks each for two pieces of evidence.* (In the case of each 2 marks, allow 1 mark for a statement and one mark for evidence from the photograph.) (b) Award *3 marks for one advantage.* (2 marks for statement and 1 mark for development.) Award *3 marks for one disadvantage.* (2 marks for statement and 1 mark for development.)
3 The local authority for this area is going to build a new shopping centre in the area shown on the photograph. (a) Identify the part of the photograph in which you would locate this shopping centre. *(2 marks)* (b) With reference to both the photograph and the map, give **one** advantage and **one** disadvantage of this location. *(8 marks)*	**3** (a) Award *2 marks for identifying a suitable location*. (b) Award *4 marks for one advantage.* (Give 2 marks for a statement, 1 mark for development and 1 mark for map/ photograph evidence.) Award *4 marks for one disadvantage.* (Give 2 marks for a statement, 1 mark for development and 1 mark for map/photographic evidence.)

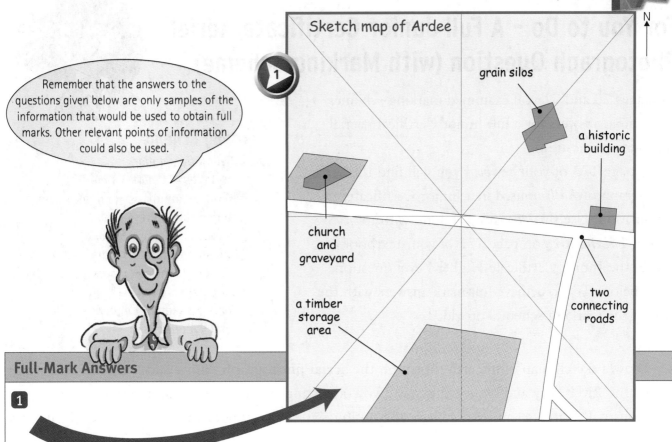

Sketch map of Ardee

N

grain silos

a historic building

church and graveyard

two connecting roads

a timber storage area

Remember that the answers to the questions given below are only samples of the information that would be used to obtain full marks. Other relevant points of information could also be used.

Full-Mark Answers

1

2 (a) (i) It is the busiest street in town. This is shown by the heavy vehicle traffic on the street in the centre middleground.

(ii) Buildings are higher here than on other streets. There are three-storey buildings on the street in the left middleground.

(b) (i) One advantage is that people living on the main street would be close to important services, such as shops and the church in the left middleground. They could easily access those services on foot.

(ii) One disadvantage is that people might be disturbed by traffic congestion, noise or air pollution from the heavy traffic, which can be seen on this street. Traffic might be a danger to children living on Main Street.

3 (a) A suitable location would be in the centre background (by the large cereal field at the edge of the town).

(b) (i) One advantage of this location is that it is connected to the town by a road. The map shows that it is also close to the N2 national primary roadway, which would provide easy access.

(ii) One disadvantage of this location is that it would mean the destruction of farmland. The photograph shows that this flat land produces cereal crops, which indicates that the land is fertile.

For You to Do – A Full Junior Certificate Aerial Photograph Question (with Marking Scheme)

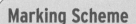

On pages 70 and 71 you examined marking schemes and sample answers for a full Junior Certificate aerial photograph question.

On page 173 of your *textbook* you will find the aerial photograph of *Ballina* used in a Junior Certificate examination. Use this *photograph* (along with the OS map of *Ballina area* on page 172 of your textbook) to answer the Junior Certificate Higher Level question given below. Try to achieve full-mark answers with the help of the marking schemes provided.

Marking Scheme

A. River Moy = *1 mark*
2 bridges = *1 mark + 1 mark*
2 connecting roads = *1 mark + 1 mark*
church with spire = *1 mark*
terraced housing = *1 mark*
industrial estate = *1 mark*
shopping centre = *1 mark*
car park = *1 mark*
shape of sketch = *2 marks*
Total = *12 marks*

★A. Draw a sketch map of the area shown on the **aerial photograph**. Show and name the following: (i) the River Moy and two bridges; (ii) two connecting streets; (iii) a church with a spire; (iv) an industrial estate; (v) an area of terraced housing; (vi) a shopping centre and car park. (*12 marks*)

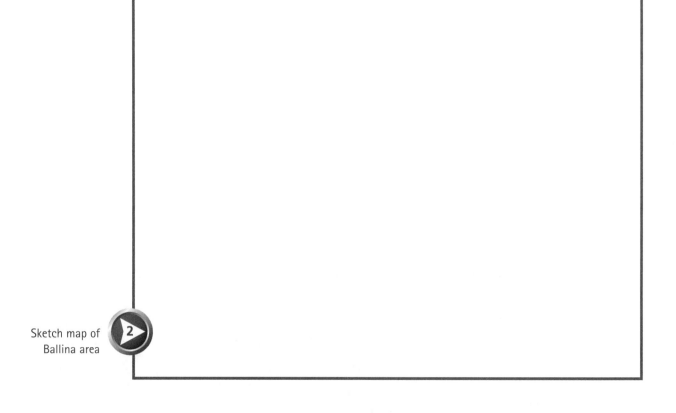

Sketch map of Ballina area ②

★B. **The town of Ballina provides a variety of services.**

With reference to the OS map only, describe three of these services. (*12 marks*)

Answers:

(i) _____

_____

_____

_____

(ii) _____

_____

_____

(iii) _____

_____

_____

> **Marking Scheme**
>
> **B.** Three descriptions at *4 marks* each.
> Allocate each *four marks* as follows:
> - *2 marks* for a statement;
> - *1 mark* for a development;
> - *1 mark* for reference to the map.
>
> **Reminder:**
> Always try to write
> *one* **extra development**
> in each description.

★C. It is proposed to redevelop the area of unused land on the right side of the river, in the right middleground of the photograph.

(i) Suggest a suitable use for this land.

(ii) Explain two reasons for your choice.

(*6 marks*)

> **Marking Scheme**
>
> **C.** (i) Give *2 marks* for a suitable land use stated.
> (ii) Give *2 marks* each for two reasons given

Answers:

(i) _____

_____

_____

(ii) • _____

_____

• _____

_____

1 Match each of the letters in **Column X** with its matching number in **Column Y**.
One match has been made for you.

Column X	
A	Natural decrease
B	Population density
C	Population explosion
D	Birth rate

Column Y	
1	The average number of people per square kilometre
2	The number of live births per 1,000 population in one year
3	When the death rate is larger than the birth rate
4	Very rapid population growth

X	Y
A	3
B	
C	
D	

2

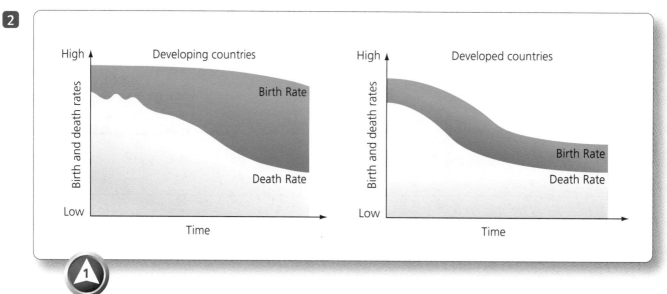

Birth rates and death rates in developing and developed countries

The statements below relate to Figure 1. Indicate whether each statement is true or false by circling the correct option.

(a) Birth rates are higher in developing than in developed countries.   *True / False*

(b) Birth rates have decreased over time, especially in developing countries.   *True / False*

(c) Natural population increase is higher in developing than in developed countries.   *True / False*

(d) In former times, death rates went up and down in developed countries.   *True / False*

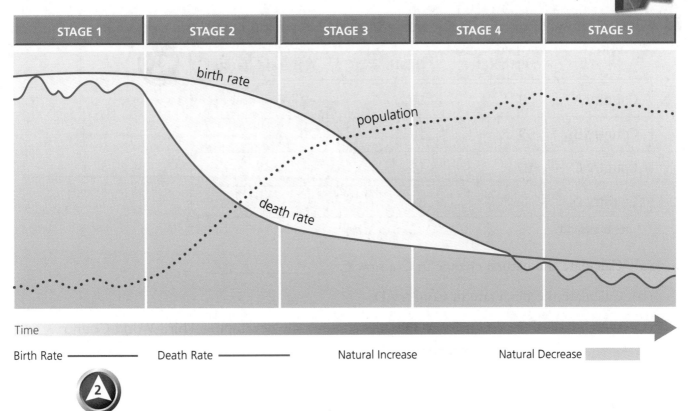

| STAGE 1 | STAGE 2 | STAGE 3 | STAGE 4 | STAGE 5 |

birth rate

population

death rate

Time

Birth Rate —————— Death Rate —————— Natural Increase Natural Decrease

A model of the population cycle

★ **3** Examine Figure 2. Then read the statements below. Not all the statements are true.

1. The diagram shows that birth rates are always higher than death rates.

2. The diagram shows that population growth is slow during Stage 1.

3. The diagram shows that population is decreasing during Stage 5.

4. The diagram shows a rapid fall in birth rates during Stage 1.

5. The diagram shows that population growth is rapid during Stage 2.

The correct statements are:

1, 2, 4 ☐   2, 3, 4 ☐   2, 3, 5 ☐   3, 4, 5 ☐   *Tick (✓) the correct box.*

★ **4** Examine Figure 2. Circle the correct answer in each of the statements below:

(a) Stage 1 is referred to as the *high fluctuating stage / low fluctuating stage*.

(b) Many Third World countries are at *Stage 3 / Stage 5* of the population cycle.

(c) Stage 4 represents the population trends in *developed countries / developing countries*.

★ 5 Figure 3 shows birth rates, death rates and natural population change in a selection of countries.

	Birth Rate*	Death Rate*	Natural Change*
Country A	8	10	−2
Country B	39	19	20
Country C	10	13	
Country D		8	0

* per thousand

(a) Calculate the natural change in Country **C**. _____

(b) Calculate the birth rate in Country **D**. _____

(c) Which one of the countries **A–D** is an economically developing Third World Country?

    _____

6 Examine the extract below and answer the questions that follow.

Birth rates and the place of women in society

Birth rates are affected by *gender /racial* issues such as the place of women in society. In places where women enjoy equality with men, women are empowered to make *more /fewer* decisions that relate to their own lives. It is clear that the empowerment of women results in *rising /falling* birth rates. In economically developed countries such as *Ireland /Uganda*, an overwhelming majority of women can choose between becoming full-time mothers and housekeepers and taking employment outside the home. This choice leads to *more /fewer* children being born. Prolonged female education also leads to *rising /falling* birth rates. Women who stay longer in education are *more /less* likely to marry young and *more /less* likely to read and be influenced by literature relating to family planning.

(a) Complete the extract by circling the *correct alternatives.*

(b) Name *four* factors, *other than* the place of women in society, that affect birth rates and/or death rates.

    • _____   • _____

    • _____   • _____

1 Examine the diagram in Figure 1, which represents the structure of the population of a small urban area.

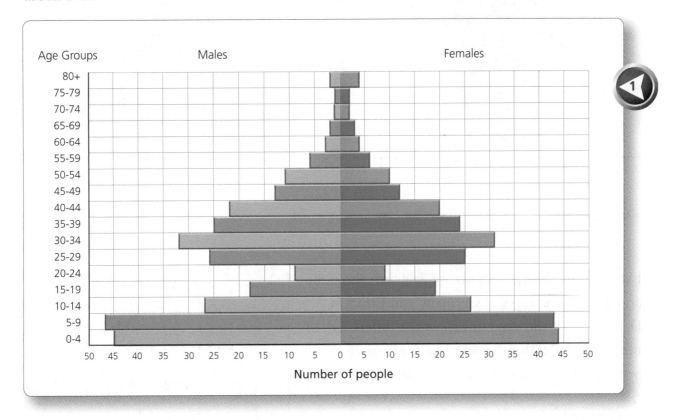

(a) What name is given to this type of diagram? _____

★ (b) How many males are there in the 0–4 age group? _____

(c) Are there more boys or girls between the ages of 10 and 14? _____

(d) How many people are there between the ages of 15 and 19? _____

(e) Does this diagram represent a fast growing or a slowly growing population?

_____

★ (f) This diagram represents an area where *young families / very old people* make up most of the population (*circle the correct option*).

(g) The area represented by this diagram might need to build more *schools / retirement homes* in the near future (*circle the correct option*).

Junior Certificate Examination Question with Marking Scheme

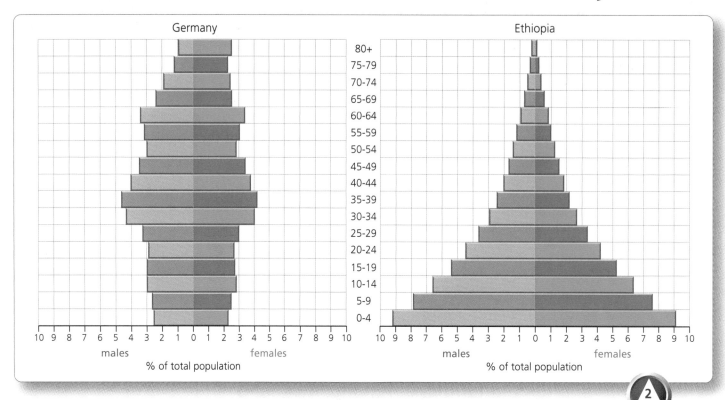

Germany

Ethiopia

80+
75-79
70-74
65-69
60-64
55-59
50-54
45-49
40-44
35-39
30-34
25-29
20-24
15-19
10-14
5-9
0-4

10 9 8 7 6 5 4 3 2 1 0 1 2 3 4 5 6 7 8 9 10

males   females

% of total population

10 9 8 7 6 5 4 3 2 1 0 1 2 3 4 5 6 7 8 9 10

males   females

% of total population

★ **2** Examine the diagrams in Figure 2, which show the population structures of Germany and Ethiopia. Describe how the diagrams show the differences in **birth rates**, **death rates** and **life expectancy** between the two countries. (*9 marks*)

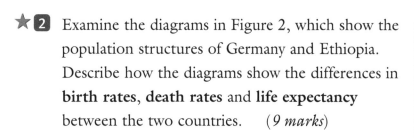

Marking Scheme

A. *Three differences (one under each heading) get 3 marks each.* Give marks as follows:
- *2 marks for statement of difference*
- *1 mark for development of statement.*

Note: Information from the pyramids must be used to get the development marks.

A sample full-mark answer is given here for 'birth rates'.

Now answer the 'death rates' and 'life expectancy' questions.

Birth rates: Birth rates are continuing to grow in Ethiopia but not in Germany.^{2} ✓ We know this because the population pyramid for Ethiopia gets wider at its base, but that of Germany gets narrower. ^{1} $\frac{3}{3}$

- **Death rates**: _____

  _____

  _____

  _____

- **Life expectancy**: _____

  _____

  _____

  _____

Reminder:
Try to write *one*
extra development
in each explanation

3 Examine Figure 3.

	Under 20	20–40	40–60	Over 80
Country A	42	32	23	3
Country B	19	29	41	11

3 Percentages of people in different age bands in two countries

(a) Does country **A** or country **B** have the greater proportion of elderly people?

  _____

(b) Which country, **A** or **B**, is more likely to be in the *North* or *First World*?

  _____

(c) Mention two economic problems that might result from a country having a large proportion of elderly people.

  - _____

    _____

  - _____

    _____

1 Match each letter in Column X with its matching number in Column Y.

	Column X
A	A person who seeks refugee status
B	A person who comes to live from another country
C	Migration from Connemara to Dublin
D	A person who leaves home to live in another country
E	Another word for 'pull factor'
F	Unemployment
G	Economic opportunities
H	The daily movement of people to and from work

	Column Y
1	A pull factor
2	Commuting
3	Rural to urban migration
4	An emigrant
5	Attractive factor
6	Immigrant
7	Asylum seeker
8	Repellent factor

A	
B	
C	3
D	
E	
F	
G	
H	

★ **2** (a) The purple area in the graph in Figure 1 represents:

population decline ☐

overpopulation ☐

static population ☐

population increase ☐

(b) Do the migration patterns shown here suggest an improving or declining Irish economy during the period shown?
Circle the correct option.
- improving economy
- declining economy

(c) *Briefly* explain your answer to question (b) by referring to the migration patterns shown.

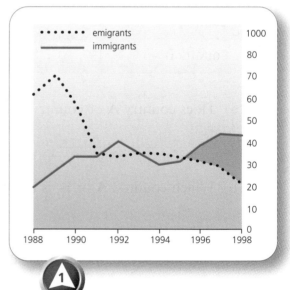

Migration patterns in Ireland

_____

_____

_____

_____

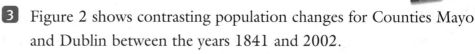

Year	Mayo	Dublin
1841	388,887	372,773
1851	274,499	405,147
1861	254,796	410,252
1871	246,030	405,262
1881	245,212	418,910
1891	219,034	419,216
1901	199,166	448,206
1911	192,177	477,196
1926	172,690	505,654
1936	161,349	586,925
1946	148,120	636,192
1951	141,867	693,022
1956	133,052	705,781
1961	123,330	718,332
1966	115,847	795,047
1971	109,525	852,219
1979	114,019	983,683
1981	114,766	1,003,164
1986	115,184	1,021,449
1991	110,713	1,025,304
1996	111,524	1,058,264
2002	117,446	1,122,821

3 Figure 2 shows contrasting population changes for Counties Mayo and Dublin between the years 1841 and 2002.

(a) What is the greatest overall *contrast* in population change between the two areas shown?

_____

_____

(b) Had Mayo or Dublin the greater population in 1841?

_____

(c) By which year had Dublin's population overtaken that of Mayo?

_____

(d) By how much did Dublin's population exceed that of Mayo in the year 2002?

_____

(e) The population figures given suggest considerable internal migration within Ireland. Has this migration been from East to West or from West to East?

_____

(f) Give *one reason* for the migration referred to in question (e) above.

_____

_____

(g) Figure 3 is a partly completed *line graph* showing *population change in Mayo between the years 1946 and 1966*. Use the figures (to the nearest thousand) in Figure 2 to complete the line graph.

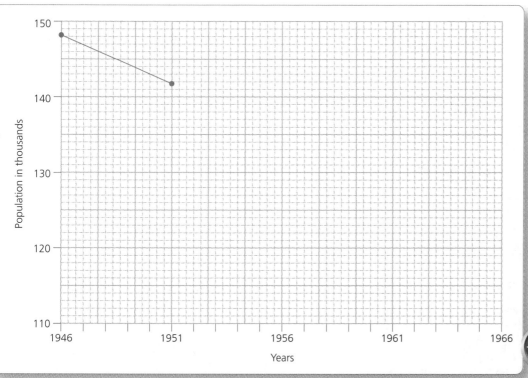

3 Population change in Mayo, 1946–1966

4 In the boxes provided in Figure 4, name two repellent (push) factors and two attractive (pull) factors that might cause people from overseas to migrate to Ireland.

PUSH FACTORS

1 _____

   _____

2 _____

   _____

PULL FACTORS

1 _____

   _____

2 _____

   _____

Sample Junior Certificate Higher Level Question with Marking Scheme

5 The *Plantation of Ulster* is an example of an organised migration. Explain three effects that this migration had on one area to which the people moved. (*9 marks*)

One effect has been written for you. Use the **Marking Scheme** provided to write full-mark answers on the other two effects.

Marking scheme:

Migration named: 1 mark
Three effects at 3 marks each
Effect one = 3 marks:
(Statement 2 marks + development 1 mark)
Effect two = 3 marks:
(Statement 2 marks + development 1 mark)
Effect three = 3 marks:
(Statement 2 marks + development 1 mark)

Reminder:
Try to write *one*
extra development
in each explanation

Full-Mark Answers

(a) The planters were English-speaking
2 ✓
Protestants. They brought a new
language and religion to Ulster. 1 ✓

(b) _____
_____
_____
_____
_____
_____

(c) _____
_____
_____
_____
_____
_____

Funtime Crossword

Clues Across

1. Migration between two countries.
6. Initials of a destination country for many Irish emigrants in the past.
8. The availability of _ _ _ _ _ _ _ _ _ might attract migrants to an area.
10. Ireland's _ _ _ _ _ _ Tiger economy offered economic opportunities to immigrants.
11. This might cause a person to become an asylum seeker.

Clues Down

2. These types of opportunities are the main cause of migration.
3. _ _ _ _ _ _ _ _ reasons; another word for 'push' factors.
4. _ _ _ _ made by governments might be a barrier to international migration.
5. An asylum seeker who has been given permission to live in another country.
6. Most internal migration is rural to _ _ _ _ _.
7. Many Irish people migrated to this east coast US city in the past.

★ **1** The **density** of a population is defined as:

the average number of people per square kilometre ☐

the total number of people in a country ☐

the number of people living in an average-sized house ☐

the age/sex structure of a rapidly growing population ☐

the extent of social inequality in a population ☐

★ **2** Look carefully at the following table (Figure 1), taken from the **2006 Census**.
It shows population change in the province of Connacht between 1981 and 2006.

Population Change in Connacht 1981-2006

	1981	1986	1991	1996	2002	2006
Galway	172,018	178,552	180,364	188,854	209,077	**231,035**
Leitrim	27,609	27,035	25,301	25,057	25,799	**28,837**
Mayo	114,766	115,184	110,713	111,524	117,446	**123,648**
Roscommon	54,543	54,592	51,697	51,975	53,774	**58,700**
Sligo	55,474	56,046	54,756	55,821	58,200	**60,863**

Source: CSO Census 2006

(a) Name the county with the largest population in 2006. _____

(b) Calculate the **increase** in population for County **Sligo** between 1981 and 2006.

_____

(c) Name the county which shows the **smallest change** in population between 1981 and 2006.

_____

(d) Galway is the only county which shows an increase in population each year. This was mainly because of the importance of Galway city. Mention **two** reasons why people migrate (move) to live in cities.

• _____

• _____

3 The map in Figure 2 shows the percentage of population that is urban in the Republic of Ireland.

(a) Tick (✓) the correct box.

    (i)   The least urbanised part of Ireland is in the east. ☐

    (ii) Connacht is more urbanised than Munster. ☑

    (iii) County Dublin is the most urbanised county. ☐

    (iv) County Cork is less urbanised than County Galway. ☐

(b) Indicate whether each of the following statements is *true* or *false* by circling the correct option.

    (i)   Between 42 and 53 per cent of the populations of Counties Cork   *True / False*
        and Kildare are urban.

    (ii) There is a higher proportion of urban dwellers in Leinster   *True / False*
        than there is in Connacht.

    (iii) Co. Limerick is more urbanised than Co. Galway.   *True / False*

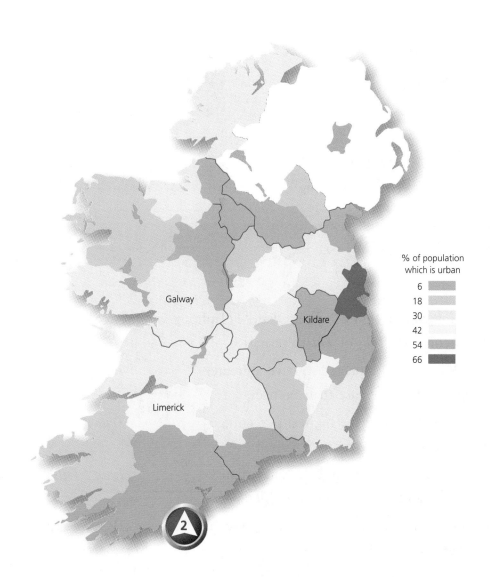

% of population
which is urban

6	
18	
30	
42	
54	
66	

★ **4** The bars in Figure 4 represent the information given in the table in Figure 3. Draw in the bars for Belgium, Ireland and Poland.

Expected population change between 2004 and 2050 in a number of countries

Table of figures

Country	Percentage change
Belgium	+5
France	+10
Italy	−9
Ireland	+36
Netherlands	+7
Poland	−12
United Kingdom	+8

Source: Irish Times, 9 April 2005

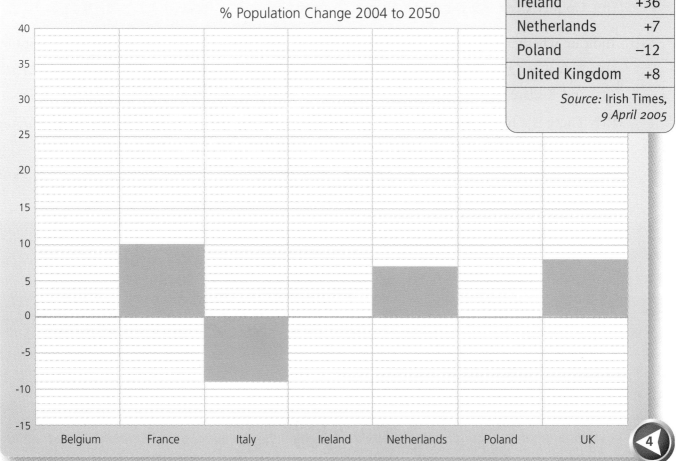

5 The following statements relate to Figures 3 and 4. Indicate whether each statement is true or false by circling the *True* or *False* alternative.

(a) The United Kingdom is expected to have a greater percentage population increase than France.   *True / False*

(b) Ireland is expected to have the highest percentage population increase of the countries named.   *True / False*

(c) France's percentage increase will be greater than those of Belgium and Netherlands combined.   *True / False*

(d) Poland's population will decrease by three per cent more than will that of Italy.   *True / False*

Chapter 33

1 Complete the following passage. Fill in the gaps by selecting words from the *selection box* provided.

Some Places with High Population Densities

Places with high population densities may suffer from problems such as overcrowding, a lack of open _____, a shortage of clean _____ and various types of pollution. Many such places can be said to be _____, which means they have too many people for the resources available to them.

Kolkata stretches along the sides of the River _____, which is a _____ of the great Ganges River. Kolkata is one of the great cities of _____ and its population is now thought to be in the region of sixteen _____ people. Many of these live in poor bustees, which have grown up along the _____ of the city. Many poor people live in overcrowded houses, or in temporary huts made from pieces of timber and _____ sheeting. About one-quarter of the people have no clean water. They have to use _____ water supplies, which are intended only for street cleaning. It is no wonder that many people suffer from _____ and other water-related diseases.

Hong Kong, which is in _____, is not as poor or as crowded as Kolkata, yet its _____ million people also suffer from overcrowding. Some people live in poor-quality high-rise apartment blocks, while others have to live in _____ in the harbour. Some industries are in new polderlands, which have been _____ from the sea. Some of Hong Kong is situated on Hong Kong Island, while other parts are in the New _____ on the mainland of China.

While cities such as Kolkata and Hong Kong suffer from overcrowding, other parts of the world are said to be _____ because they do not have enough people to develop their resources fully. Places with very low population densities often suffer from _____ marriage rates, from the _____ of agricultural land and from political and economic _____. The country of _____ in West Africa and the _____ of Ireland are two areas with low population densities.

Selection Box

- edges
- distributary
- Mali
- Territories
- space
- houseboats
- reclaimed
- China
- plastic
- West
- million
- dysentery
- abandonment
- unfiltered
- low
- isolation
- overpopulated
- underpopulated
- seven
- water
- India
- Hooghly

2 The picture shows a street scene in a densely populated city that was described in Chapter **33** of your textbook.

(a) Name the city and the country in which it is situated.

- City: _____

- Country: _____

(b) Under the headings below, describe the social and economic effects of very high population density in the city shown in the picture.

- **Overcrowding:** _____

_____

_____

_____

_____

- **Shortage of clean water:** _____

_____

_____

_____

_____

- **Pollution:** _____

_____

_____

_____

_____

3 The country shown in colour in Figure 1 has a very low human population density.

★ (a) Name the country.

_____

(b) Attempt to explain *why* population density is higher in the 'higher density' part of the country shown than it is in the 'very low density' part of the country.

THE SAHEL

ALGERIA

very low density
less than 1 person per km²

medium density
1–24 people per km²

higher density
over 24 people per km²

MAURITANIA

NIGER

Timbuktu

Mopti

Ségou   San

Bamako

Bia

BURKINA
FASO

River Niger

1

_____
_____
_____
_____
_____

★ (c) Describe *two* problems caused by low population density that affect the country shown.

● _____
_____
_____
_____
_____

● _____
_____
_____
_____
_____

1 The map shows average daily calorie intakes in different countries.

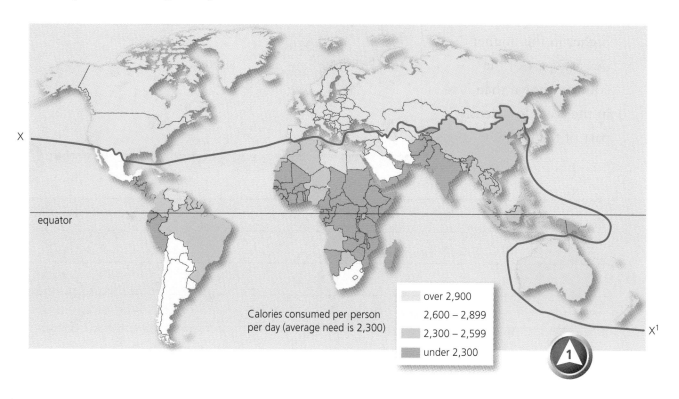

★ (a) Write down the daily calorie intake per person in each of the following countries:

 • Ireland _____   • Brazil _____   • India _____

★ (b) What name is given to that part of the world beneath the line marked X–X¹?

_____

(c) Name two First World countries that are located south of the Equator.

 • _____

 • _____

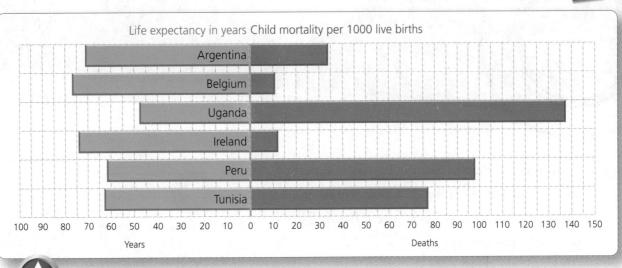

Life expectancy in years Child mortality per 1000 live births

| | |
Argentina, Belgium, Uganda, Ireland, Peru, Tunisia

100 90 80 70 60 50 40 30 20 10 0 10 20 30 40 50 60 70 80 90 100 110 120 130 140 150

Years   Deaths

2 Life expectancy and child mortality rates

★**2** (a) Judging by the information given in the graphs above:

(i) Which of the countries named is the most developed?

_____

(ii) Which of the countries named is the least developed?

_____

(iii) What is meant by the term *child mortality rate*?

_____

_____

Marking Scheme

(a) (i) *1 mark* for correct country named
(ii) *1 mark* for correct country named
(iii) *2 marks* for full, clear definition

(b) Two reasons at *3 marks* each. (In each case give *two marks* for a statement and *1 mark* for a development.)

(c) *2 marks:* one for each *true/false* option identified correctly.

(b) Give *two* reasons why life expectancy rates are higher in First World countries than they are in Third World countries.

● _____

_____

● _____

_____

(c) Indicate whether each of the following statements is true or false by circling one of the *True / False* options:

● Ireland has a life expectancy rate of 74 years and has the lowest child mortality rate of the countries shown.   *True / False*

● Uganda has a lower life expectancy rate than has Tunisia.   *True / False*

1 (a) Examine the map in Figure 1, which shows Norman towns in Ireland. These towns are situated mainly in which of the following parts of the country?

Tick (✓) the correct box.

- The North and East ☐
- The South and East ☐
- The North and West ☐
- The South and West ☐

(b) Give *two reasons* why most Norman towns were located in the parts of the country you identified in question (a) above.

- _____
  _____
- _____
  _____

2 Figure 2 shows part of a street map of Kilkenny City. What evidence on the map suggests that the area shown was part of a medieval Norman town?

_____
_____
_____
_____

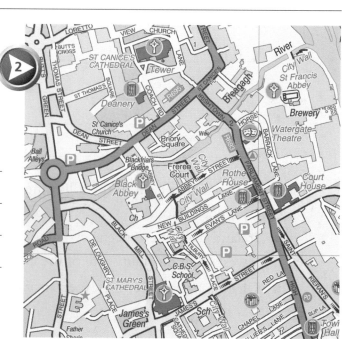

3 In the case of any *one* named Norman settlement in Ireland, explain in as much detail as possible how the location of the settlement was influenced by each of the following:

Name of settlement: _____

- *Where its Norman settlers came from* _____

_____

- *Availability of water* _____

_____

- *Availability of food* _____

_____

- *Communications* _____

_____

- *A means of defence* _____

_____

Wordwheels

4 Insert the missing letters to complete the names of two important Norman towns in Ireland. Each name can read clockwise or anticlockwise.

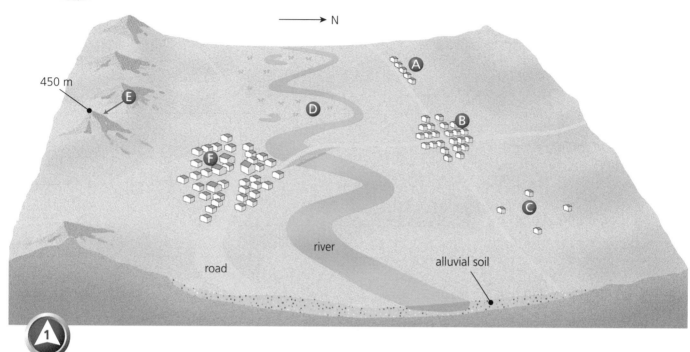

1   Examine the sketch map showing settlement in Figure 1 above.

   (a) *Name the settlement pattern* at each of the places labelled **A**, **B** and **C** on the sketch map.

        A _____

        B _____

        C _____

   (b) Give *one reason* why there is no settlement at the place labelled **D**.

        _____

   (c) Give *two reasons* why there is no settlement at **E**.

        1 _____

        2 _____

   (d) Give *two reasons* why the town labelled **F** may have developed where it did.

        1 _____

        2 _____

Chapter 36

2 Draw a circle around the correct alternative in each of the statements below.

> *'Random pattern' means no particular pattern.

(a) The term 'settlement pattern' refers to the way in which *settlements grow / are arranged / are modified*.

(b) Viking towns were usually distributed in a *random* / *linear* / *dispersed* pattern along the *south and east* / *north and west* coasts of Ireland.

(c) Early Norman settlements tended to be *clustered* / *scattered* throughout Ireland, but were especially common in the *west* / *east* / *north* of the country.

(d) Settlements along a road or at the foot of a hill are usually arranged in a *dispersed* / *linear* / *nucleated* pattern.

3 The map in Figure 2 shows the locations of some nucleated settlements.

(a) Are these settlements distributed in a generally *nucleated*, *ribboned* or *dispersed* pattern?

_____

(b) Explain in one sentence *why* these settlements are distributed in the pattern you identified in (a) above.

_____

_____

(c) Which of the settlements shown is at the lowest bridging point of the River Suir?

_____

(d) Why are important settlements often located at the lowest bridging points of rivers?

_____

_____

_____

★ **1** (a) Areas of land reclaimed from the sea are called:

   polders ☐   favelas ☐

   colonies ☐   lagoons ☐

(b) Ridges of high ground that separate polders from the sea are called:

   canals ☐   drainage ditches ☐

   dykes ☐   sea walls ☐

(c) *Rural* settlement patterns in the Dutch polders tend to be:

   linear along the sides of roads ☐

   nucleated in the centre of polders ☐

   random throughout the polders ☐

   linear along the sea shore ☐

★ **2** Examine the map of a European country in Figure 1. Indicate whether each of the statements below is true or false by circling the '*True*' or '*False*' option.

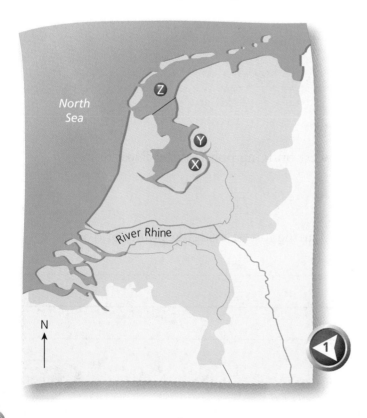

(a) The country shown is Belgium.

   True / False

(b) The area labelled 'X' is an example of a polder.

   True / False

(c) The River Rhine flows generally westwards through the country.

   True / False

(d) The area labelled 'Y' is the North East Polder.

   True / False

(e) The map shows that the River Rhine flows through part of Germany.

   True / False

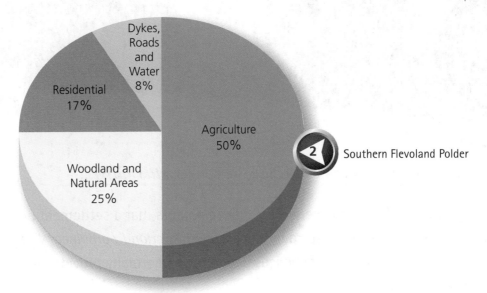

Agriculture 50%

Residential 17%

Dykes, Roads and Water 8%

Woodland and Natural Areas 25%

2 Southern Flevoland Polder

3 Look at the pie chart in Figure 2 above.
Circle the correct answer in *each* of the following statements:

- In Southern Flevoland, *one-quarter / one-half* of the land is used for agriculture.

- In Southern Flevoland, *one-quarter / one-third* of the land is woodland and natural areas.

- In Southern Flevoland, the amount of residential land is *greater than / smaller than* the amount of woodland and natural areas.

4 Examine the sketch map of the North East Polder in Figure 3.
(a) Name the principal town labelled **A**.

_____

(b) What are the features labelled **1–9**?

_____

(c) On the sketch map join with a line the features labelled **1–9**. What does this line represent?

_____

(d) On the sketch map join each of the features **1–9** with the principal town. What does each of those lines represent?

_____

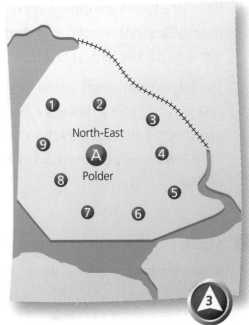

North-East
A
Polder

(e) Indicate whether each of the following statements is true or false.
(Circle the correct *True / False* option.)

- The settlement shown in Figure 3 is a planned settlement.   *True / False*
- The settlement pattern shown is a ribboned settlement.   *True / False*

1 Complete the following passage by circling the correct *alternatives*.

The term 'functions' refers to the *services / entertainments* that a settlement provides for its people and for the people of the surrounding area or *hinterland / province*. Villages usually provide a *great / limited* number of services. Large towns normally provide more *general / specialised* services than villages do.

Some old towns developed near medieval castles that helped to provide a *resource / defence* function for those towns. An example of such a town on the Shannon Basin is *Athlone / Shannonbridge*. The term 'river basin' refers to the area of land that is *flooded / drained* by a river and its tributaries.

Some settlements have or had ecclesiastical functions because they served the *religious / commercial* needs of their people. The city of *Köln / Rotterdam* on the *Rhine / Danube* basin is such a city and has a very famous Gothic cathedral that dates from *Ancient Roman times / the Middle Ages*.

Resource towns are often built near *roads / mines* that provide natural resources. The city of *Essen / Basle* developed as a resource settlement in the Rhine Basin. The Rhine Basin also has many ports, the largest of which is *Basle / Rotterdam*.

The largest settlement in the Shannon Basin is *Athlone / Limerick*. It was begun by the *Normans / Vikings* and had a defence function for many centuries. This settlement now has a recreational function. Its cultural attractions include the *Hunt Museum / National Museum* and the *Bell Table / Top Table* theatre. Limerick city hotels provide approximately *350 / 3,500 / 35,000* rooms for tourists.

2 Match each letter in Column X with the number of its pair in Column Y.

Column X	
A	Castles and city walls
B	Docks
C	Housing estates
D	Stores, fairs, co-operative marts
E	Large quarries, mines or bogs

Column Y	
1	Market function
2	Defence function
3	Resource function
4	Residential function
5	Port function

X	Y
A	
B	
C	
D	
E	

3 Examine the map of the Shannon Basin in Figure 1. Identify each of the settlements, rivers or lakes labelled **1–18**. Use them to complete the word puzzle attached to Figure 1.

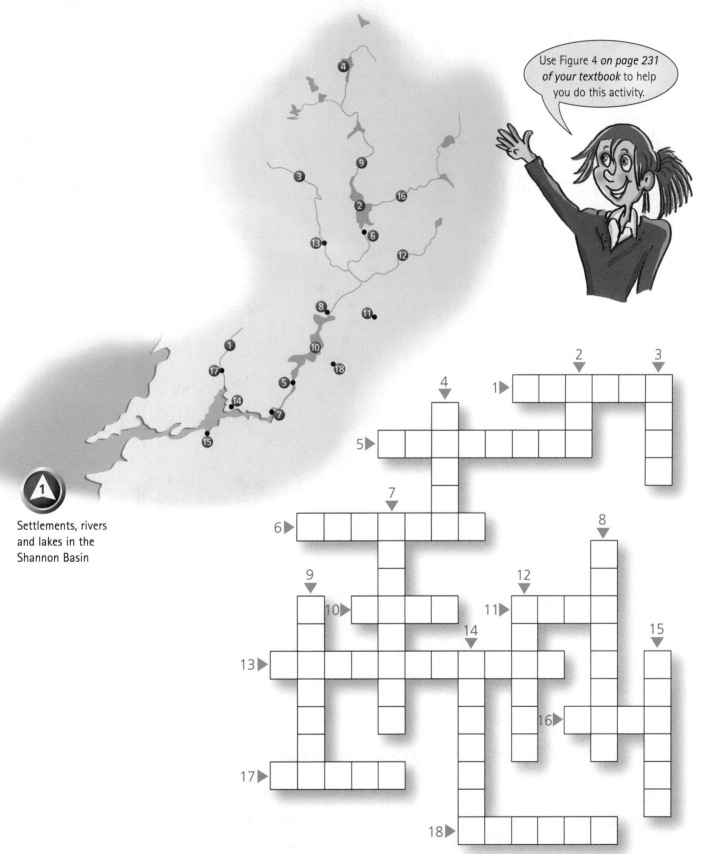

Settlements, rivers and lakes in the Shannon Basin

Use Figure 4 *on page 231 of your textbook* to help you do this activity.

4 (a) Examine the map of the Rhine Basin in Figure 2. In the spaces provided name the countries **1–4**, the rivers **5–8** and the cities **9–14**.

You can use Figure 8 *on page 234 of your textbook* to help you.

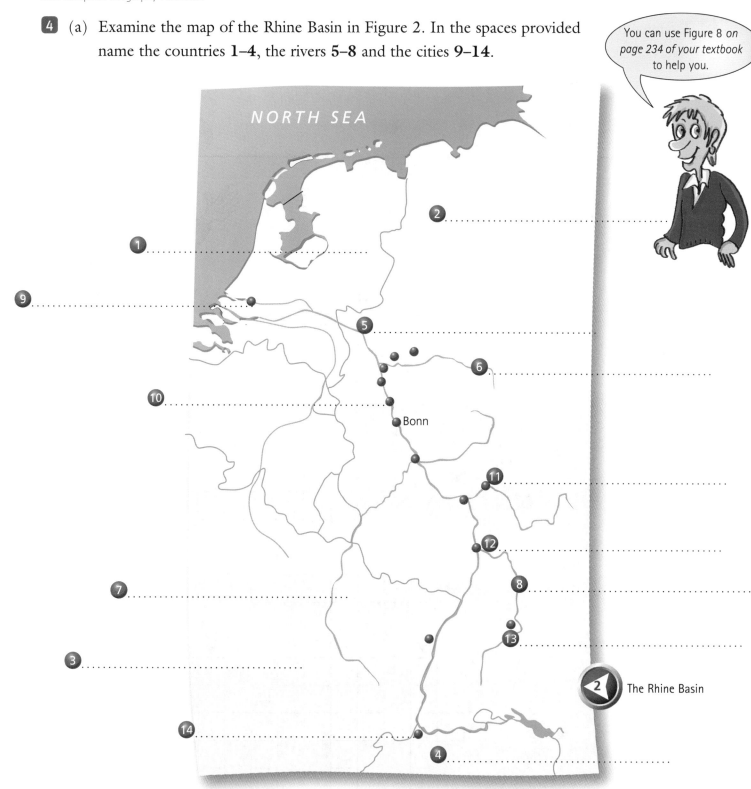

NORTH SEA

Bonn

The Rhine Basin

(b) In the boxes provided, name *one* principal function of *each* city named below.

City	Function
● Rotterdam	
● Essen	
● Köln	

City	Function
● Dortmund	
● Bonn	
● Basle	

5 In the spaces provided, describe three functions of *Limerick City* and three functions of *Köln*. Use the marking scheme given below to guide you.

Marking Scheme

Each function is awarded *four marks*, which are allocated as follows:

- Naming the function = *1 mark*
- Development = *2 marks*
- Example or other development = *1 mark*

Try to write *one* **extra** development for each description.

For Example:

Limerick has a major residential function. ¹✓ Many of its people now live in suburbs at the edges of the city. ²✓ Ballynanty ⁺¹ is an example of such a suburb. $\frac{4}{4}$

Limerick City	Köln
1	1
2	2
3	3

1 In the grid provided, match each of the features or characteristics in Column X with its matching town function in Column Y. One match has been made for you.

Column X (features or characteristics)	
A	Castles
B	Fertile agricultural hinterland*
C	Mineral resources
D	Cathedrals and churches
E	Sheltered harbour
F	Industrial estate

Column Y (town functions)	
1	Ecclesiastical
2	Market
3	Manufacturing
4	Defence
5	Mining
6	Port

X	Y
A	
B	
C	
D	
E	
F	

*hinterland = surrounding area

2 Which of the following statements are true?

1. The functions of towns may change over time.

2. Towns such as Navan and Dungarvan are multifunctional.

3. People often commute between dormitory towns and nearby cities where they work.

4. Navan is a mining town in Co. Cavan.

5. Dungarvan is a thriving port in Co. Waterford.

6. Manufacturing has played a role in the development of Dungarvan.

The correct statements are:

1, 2, 4 and 5 ☐   1, 2, 3 and 5 ☐   1, 2, 3 and 6 ☐   2, 3, 4 and 6 ☐

Tick (✓) the correct box.

Junior Certificate Question with Marking Scheme

3 **Question**: *The function of a town may change over time.*

   (a) Name a town that you have studied whose function has changed.

   (b) Describe and explain the changes in function that have taken place. *(10 marks)*

Sample Full-Mark Answer

We have studied the changing functions of Navan. **1 ✓**

1 Navan was an important walled town in Norman times. **2 ✓**
Its defensive function lasted until the sixteenth century. **1 ✓**

2 As time went on, Navan developed as a market town. **2 ✓**
It has a rich agricultural hinterland with rich limestone-based soils. **1 ✓**

3 Navan later became a resource (mining) settlement. **2 ✓**
Tara Mines employs hundreds of people extracting and processing zinc. **1 ✓**

Marking Scheme

A town named = *1 mark*
Three different functions over time at 3 marks each.
For each function: statement = 2 + development = 1

> Now answer the question below using the same marking scheme. To ensure full marks, try to write one **extra development** for each explanation.

Question: Choose any named town that you have studied, other than Navan, and describe three ways in which its function has changed over time.

Name of town: _____

(a) _____
_____
_____

(b) _____
_____
_____

(c) _____
_____
_____

1 Link each of the letters in Column X with its matching number in Column Y.
One match has been made.

Column X	
A	*Rhine-Rhone* and *Main-Danube*
B	The main hub (meeting place) of Irish road and rail routes
C	Called 'the main road of Germany'
D	A means of transporting information
E	Used to reduce congestion in urban areas
F	Information Age Town

Column Y	
1	Ring roads
2	Rhine
3	Ennis
4	Dublin
5	Canals
6	Telecom

X	Y
A	
B	
C	
D	
E	1
F	

2 Indicate whether each of the statements below is *true* or *false* by circling the correct *alternative* in each case.

(a) The Rhine rises in Switzerland, flows through much of Germany and enters the North Sea in the Netherlands. *True / False*

(b) The Rhine has its source in the Netherlands and much of its course in Germany. *True / False*

(c) The Upper Rhine is in Switzerland and the Lower Rhine is in the Netherlands. *True / False*

(d) In general, ships and barges carry raw materials down the Rhine and industrial goods up the Rhine. *True / False*

(e) Port cities in the Netherlands, Germany and Switzerland are all linked by Rhine water transport. *True / False*

(f) Information technology is capable of linking settlements in all parts of the world. *True / False*

Chapter 40

Giant Revision Wordgame for Chapters 38 to 40

Clues Down

A. Source country of the River Rhine.

B. People live in this type of town but work in a nearby city.

Clues Across

1. Might be evidence of an old defence town.
2. Munster city
3. Area surrounding a settlement – see page 104 of workbook
4. A business that can be run equally well in many different places
5. German for 'confluence' and a city on the Rhine
6. 'Information Age Town' in Co. Clare
7. Large lake on the River Shannon
8. The Main-Danube is one
9. Tributary that joins the Rhine at Koblenz
10. Home of the Dutch
11. Dungarvan engineering company
12. Important market, port and recreational city on the Rhine
13. An Irish settlement with a co-operative mart would have this function
14. *Sounds* like the principal tributary of the Rhine
15. City at the lowest bridge point of the Shannon
16. Europe's largest port
17. Town on the Shannon below Lough Ree
18. These people developed Limerick City in medieval times
19. Might be found in a settlement with an old ecclesiastical function

★ **1** Which of the following statements best describes the information shown in the cartoon?

(a) Dublin City is constantly attracting new residents from outlying areas. ☐

(b) Dublin City looks like a saucer-shaped depression. ☐

(c) New towns outside Dublin have taken the overspill population from the city. ☐

(d) Tallaght is continually decreasing in population size. ☐

Tick (✓) the correct box.

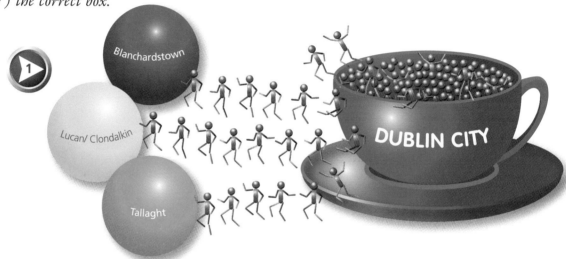

2 Figure 2 shows the populations in 1994 and the expected populations in 2015 of the world's largest cities. Using the information in Figure 2, name each of the following:

(a) The largest city in 1994.

_____

(b) The fourth largest city in 2015.

_____

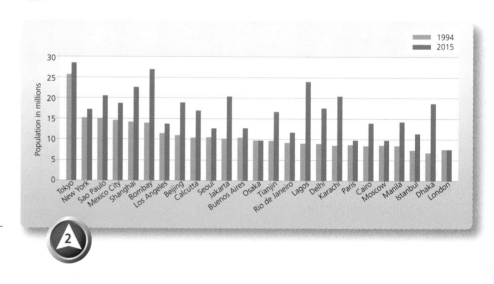

(c) The city expected to show the greatest population growth between 1994 and 2015.

_____

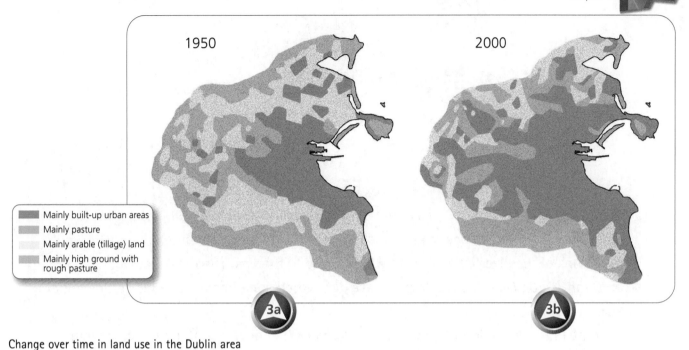

Change over time in land use in the Dublin area

3 The statements 1-5 below refer to Figures 3a and 3b. Not all of the statements are true.

1. Agricultural land has decreased over time.

2. Rough pasture continues to be an important land use to the north of the city.

3. The amount of pasture has increased over time.

4. Built-up urban areas have increased in the west.

5. Urbanisation has increased greatly over time.

The correct statements are numbers:

1, 2, 3 ☐   1, 2, 4 ☐   1, 4, 5 ☐   2, 4, 5 ☐

4 Dublin grew rapidly during the nineteenth and twentieth centuries. Give three reasons for this, using the headings below:

• *Administrative reason:* _____

  _____

• *Economic reason:* _____

  _____

• *Social reason:* _____

  _____

New Complete Geography Workbook

5

Complete the passage below by circling the correct option in each of the alternatives given.

The Development of Dublin over Time

The growth of urban areas – also called *decentralisation /urbanisation* – has affected Dublin over time. Dublin began as a small *Viking /Norman* settlement on the *north / south* bank of the River *Liffey /Lee*. It was referred to then as 'The Black Pool' or *Lon Dubh /Dubh Linn*. Archaeologists have discovered some remains of this settlement at *Pope's Quay /Wood Quay*.

By the fourteenth century, the *Vikings /Normans* had developed Dublin into a large *medieval /Renaissance* city surrounded by a defensive high wall. As well as being an important *port /university* town, Dublin had by that time become the *mining / administrative* centre of Ireland. At this time, Dublin's streets were *narrow /wide* and *dark /well lit*. Fishamble Street was so called because it was in *very poor repair / where people sold fish*. But Dublin did not grow steadily at this time. Disasters such as the *Great Flood /Black Death* reduced the population greatly.

Dublin developed into one of Europe's most splendid cities during the *Georgian / Edwardian* period. Most of the old medieval walls were *rebuilt /demolished* and wide new streets such as *Cook Street /O'Connell Street* were built. Places such as *Merrion Square /The Liberties* were known for their fine *multi-storey /single-storey* Georgian houses; while manufacturing industry thrived in *Merrion Square /The Liberties*.

The nineteenth century saw the *establishment /abolition* of the Irish Parliament and this caused Dublin *to develop further /to decline* as a centre of administration and fashion. Many Georgian areas *decayed /were improved*. Rich people moved to new suburbs such as *Lucan /Dalkey*, which by the end of the century were linked to the city by *new roads /railway lines*.

In recent times, Dublin has grown very rapidly indeed. It is Ireland's *private /primate* city. This means that it is more than *twice /twenty* times the size of the next largest city in the Republic of Ireland, which is *Galway /Cork*. Dublin is surrounded by many *dormitory / dormer* towns. As more and more agricultural land is *re-zoned /renewed* to allow for the building of suburbs, Dublin is gradually spreading into adjoining counties such as *Wexford /Kildare*. This has resulted in the swallowing up of small villages and in other problems associated with *urban decay /urban sprawl*.

110

★ **1** Which of the following would you *not* expect to find in a typical Western city?

industrial areas ☐   a number of shopping centres ☐

residential areas ☐   many houses built in an unplanned way ☐

a central core area of business ☐

★ **2** Use the lines numbered 1, 2 and 3 to label the divided rectangle in Figure 1.
Refer to the information given in the pie chart in Figure 2.
Two labels have been added for you.

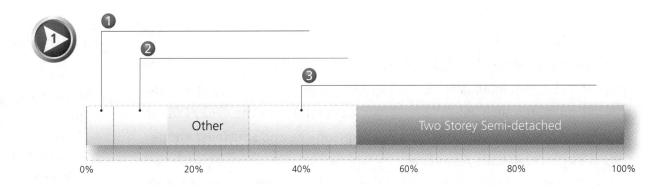

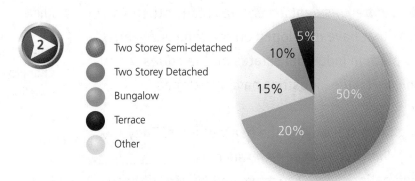

★ **3** The sketch map in Figure 3 contains four labelled functional zones in an imaginary large town in Ireland.

Match each of the labels **A–D** on the map with its matching pair from the four functional zones listed in the table in Figure 4. One pair has been completed for you.

Legend:
- Motorway
- Other main roads
- ✈ Airport
- Suburban area

Functional zone	Matching label (letter)
CBD	
Older residential (housing) area	
Newer residential area	
Industrial estate	A

4 Select *some* of the words or phrases from the selection box to complete the passage below on Paris. Also select the correct *alternatives* by crossing out the incorrect options.

Functional Zones in Paris

The Central Business District of Paris is located at the *edge /centre* of the city. It includes famous streets such as the _____ and landmark public buildings such as _____ Cathedral. Like the *CBD /CDB* of any great city, it contains many banks, large offices and specialist shops such as *grocery shops /jewellers*.

Paris has several smaller shopping areas outside of its main CBD. Some of these were the urban centres of places such as _____ and St _____, before they became swallowed up by a growing Paris.

Most people live in *the city centre /residential suburbs*. Many others live in large *tourist /satellite* towns that have developed on the fringes of Paris.

Most manufacturing takes place in industrial estates *on the edges / at the heart* of the city. *Chemical /textile* industries have developed in dockside locations along the River _____.

Most /a few manufacturing firms still exist in the heart of Paris. They make *expensive luxury items /cheap consumer items* such as _____.

Paris has many open air recreation areas. The most well known of these include the *Luxembourg* _____ and the *Bois de France / Bois de Boulogne*.

Selection Box
- Rouen
- Christ the King
- Seine
- Gardens
- Garden furniture
- Versailles
- Villas
- Notre Dame
- Pierre
- Rhine
- Denis
- Rue St Louis
- Champs Elysées
- Jewellery

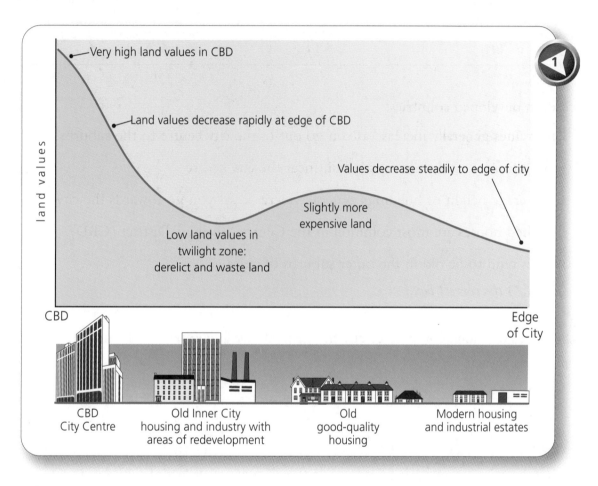

Very high land values in CBD

Land values decrease rapidly at edge of CBD

Values decrease steadily to edge of city

Slightly more expensive land

Low land values in twilight zone: derelict and waste land

land values

CBD

Edge of City

CBD City Centre

Old Inner City housing and industry with areas of redevelopment

Old good-quality housing

Modern housing and industrial estates

★ **1** Study the diagram, which shows a cross-section of a city.

You are required to identify which *three* of these statements are correct.

1. Land values in the city centre are very high.

2. Land values are lowest at the edge of the city.

3. Two-storey buildings are found mainly in the city centre.

4. Values rise in the zone of modern housing and industrial estates.

5. In the old inner city land values are relatively low.

The *correct* statements are numbers:

1, 3, 5 ☐   1, 2, 5 ☐   2, 3, 4 ☐   3, 4, 5 ☐

2 Look again at Figure 1 on page 113.

★   (a) State which part of the city has the highest land values. _____

★   (b) Give two explanations of why land values are high in that part of the city.

● _____

_____

● _____

_____

★ **3** In cities in developed countries:

● land values generally increase as you go out of the city centre to the suburbs ☐

● new industrial estates are mostly built near the city centre ☐

● the average height of buildings generally increases as you go towards the city centre ☐

● detached houses are most common in the Central Business District (CBD) ☐

● houses tend to be old in the outer suburbs of cities ☐

Tick (✓) the correct box.

4 In the boxes provided compare briefly the general *type* and *intensity* of land use in the three urban zones shown.

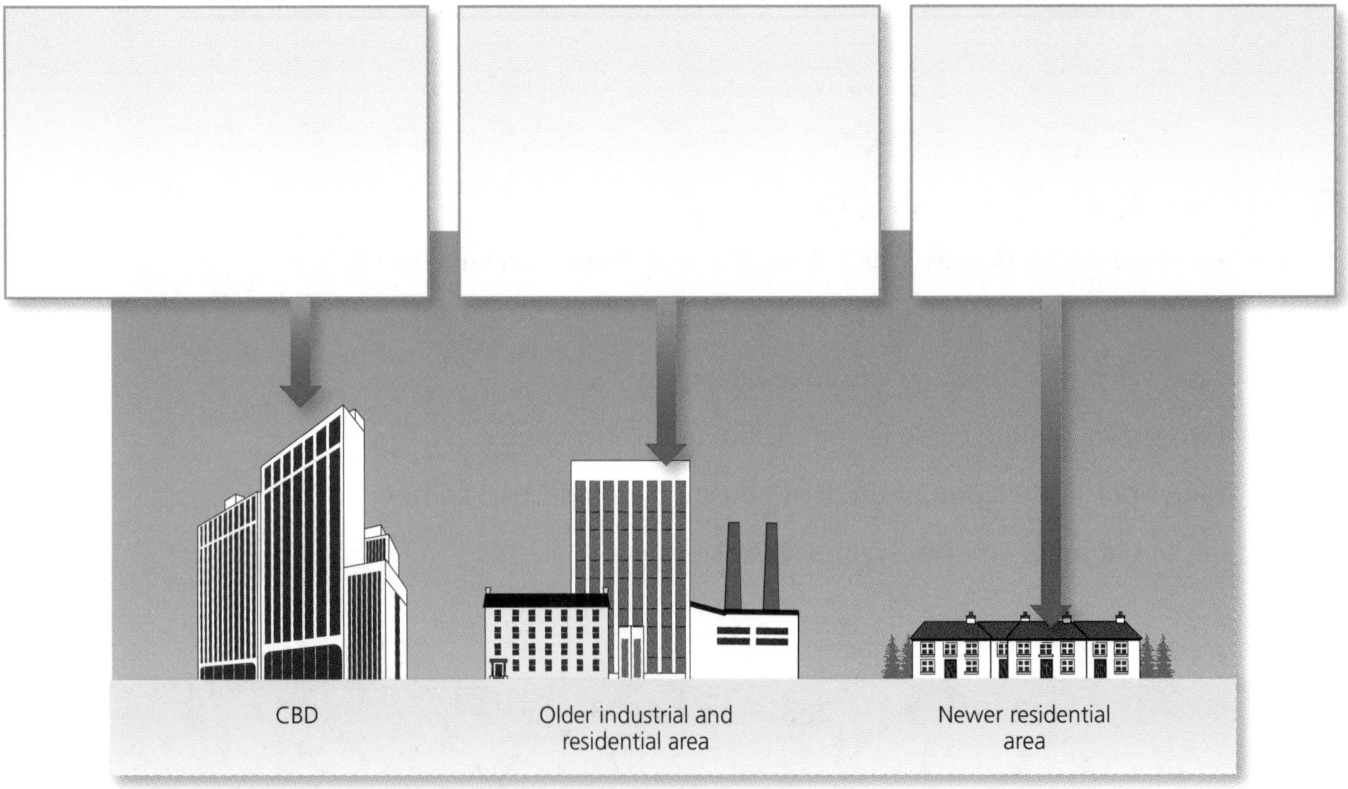

CBD   Older industrial and residential area   Newer residential area

5 Examine the photographs of Irish urban dwellings labelled A to E. The statements below relate to these photographs. Indicate whether each statement is true or false by circling the *True* or *False* option.

(a) The lowest density dwelling is shown in photograph A.

True / False

(b) The houses in photograph C are older than those in photograph E.

True / False

(c) The house in photograph A has more floor space than has a house in photograph C.

True / False

(d) The houses in photograph D are in an area of lower density than those in photograph E.

True / False

(e) The houses in photograph C are likely to be nearer to the city centre than those in photograph E.

True / False

(f) Housing densities are highest in the dwellings shown in photograph B.

True / False

(g) The houses in photograph D appear to have been built by a City Council or other public authority.

True / False

(h) Land values in photograph A are lower than those in photograph B.

True / False

(i) Houses in photograph E are likely to be located in an inner city area.

True / False

Chapter 45

1 (a) The bar graph in Figure 1 shows the number of vehicles that entered and left an Irish settlement on a certain day. Complete the bar graphs so as to show *each* of the following pieces of information:

- 60 vehicles entered the settlement between 15.00 and 16.00 hours
- 240 vehicles left the settlement between 17.00 and 18.00 hours
- 80 vehicles entered the settlement between 18.00 and 19.00 hours

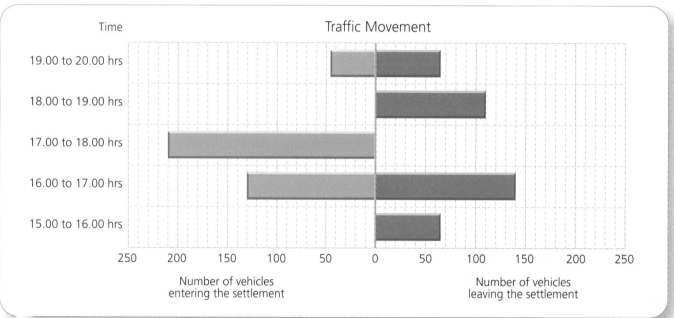

(b) What was the hour of peak traffic flow in the settlement referred to in Figure 1?

_____

(c) Suggest why the hour identified in (b) above was the hour of peak traffic flow.

_____

_____

2 Study the diagram in Figure 2, which shows percentage increases in the time it took to travel to Dublin City between 1990 and 2006.

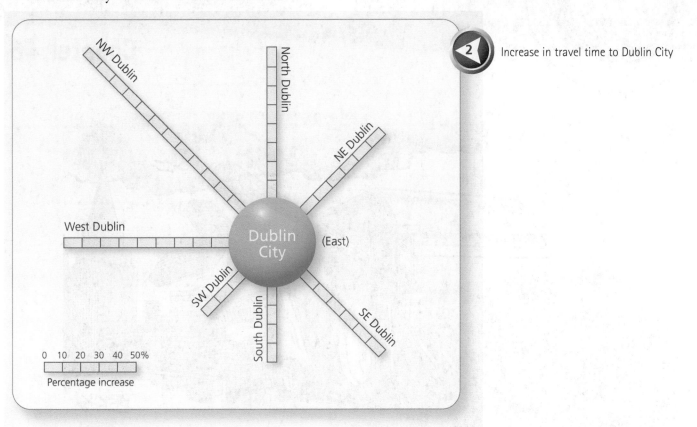

(a) Name, *in rank order*, the three areas worst affected by the increase in travel times.

(i) _____

(ii) _____

(iii) _____

(b) What is the percentage increase in travel time to the city from North East Dublin?

_____

(c) Why do you think no increase in travel time is recorded from the East?

_____

(d) Explain *two* actions that could be taken to reduce delays in travel time in and out of Dublin.

(i) _____

_____

(ii) _____

★ **1** The statement that best describes the situation in the cartoon in Figure 1 is:

more land is needed for agriculture ☐

urban development is carefully planned ☐

urban development rolls on at the expense of farmland ☐

suburban housing estates are located at the edge of the cities ☐

★ **2** **Urban sprawl** is:

the spread of a city into the surrounding countryside ☐

a rapid increase in the number of tall buildings in a city ☐

the growth of a city's traffic ☐

the fast growth of a city's population ☐

3 Name *three* problems associated with urban sprawl.

(a) _____

(b) _____

(c) _____

4 Name *three* problems associated with **urban decline**.

(a) _____

(b) _____

(c) _____

5 Examine the statements 1 to 8 below. Indicate which group of statements is correct by ticking the appropriate box.

1. Transport, recreational and educational facilities are all part of the infrastructural services of an urban area.

2. In 2007, up to 200 people in Limerick City became ill owing to polluted water supplies.

3. There are plans to build large waste incinerators at Ringaskiddy near Cork City and at Poolbeg in Dublin.

4. Adequate recreational facilities now exist in all major Irish suburban areas.

5. Inadequate public transport has led to traffic congestion in our cities.

6. Urban sprawl has swallowed up former villages such as Douglas in Dublin and Dundrum in Cork.

7. Urban redevelopment in Ireland has taken place mostly in the outer suburbs of our cities.

8. Urban decline occurs mainly on the fringes of Irish cities.

The correct statements are:

1, 2, 7 ☐

1, 3, 5 ☐

2, 5, 8 ☐

3, 5, 6 ☐

4, 5, 8 ☐

5, 6, 7 ☐

Chapter 47

1 Examine the cartoon in Figure 1. Which of the following processes does the cartoon show?

Urban sprawl ☐

Rural to urban migration ☐

Urban redevelopment ☐

Urban renewal ☐

Tick (✓) the correct box.

2 In western cities many planning authorities have tried to overcome social and economic problems. Cross out the incorrect words in these statements.

- Rates and taxes have been *increased / decreased* as an incentive for developers.
- High-rise apartments have been *encouraged / discouraged*.
- Older houses have been *preserved / replaced* by new buildings.

3 Link each of the letters in Column X with its matching number in Column Y.

	Column X		Column Y		
A	Inner city housing areas converted to office blocks	1	Tallaght	A	
B	Inner city houses refurbished for existing families	2	Greenhills	B	
C	Fatima Mansions	3	Examples of 'new towns'	C	
D	Tramway service in Dublin	4	Urban renewal	D	
E	Blanchardstown and Shannon	5	Urban redevelopment	E	
F	An industrial estate in Tallaght	6	Luas	F	
G	Built to house 'overspill' city population	7	A renewed area in Dublin	G	

Junior Certificate Higher Level Question with Marking Scheme

4 *'Urban renewal, urban redevelopment and new towns are all used by planners to reduce problems of modern city life.'*

★ (a) Examine the newspaper extract provided here and state whether it refers to urban renewal or to urban redevelopment.

_____

★ (b) Briefly describe one difference between urban renewal and urban redevelopment.

_____

_____

_____

_____

_____

Newspaper Extract:
Dublin Corporation is trying to persuade people in parts of the old Liberties area of the inner city not to abandon their old neighbourhoods. With this in mind, many houses are being restored by the Corporation and new community services are being provided in the area.

Marking Scheme
(a) Write renewal or redevelopment = *2 marks*
(b) Make one statement about renewal (*2 marks*) and one statement about redevelopment (*2 marks*) which show the *difference* between them = *4 marks*
(c) Name any new town in Ireland = *2 marks*
(d) Two descriptions at 2 marks each = *4 marks*
(e) Two problems named at 1 mark each = *2 marks*

★ (c) Name any New Town in Ireland.

_____

★ (d) Briefly describe two typical features of this New Town.

● _____

_____

● _____

_____

(e) Which problems are (i) urban renewal and (ii) new towns designed to reduce?

(i) _____

(ii) _____

A New Scheme of Urban Renewal for Parts of Limerick City

Housing estates in the Limerick City suburbs of Moyross, Southill and Ballinacurra Weston have for years been in the news for the wrong reasons. Dogged by high unemployment, some residents of these estates have been harassed and even driven from their homes by criminal minorities. Their houses have been vandalised and occasionally burned.

In 2008, the Government announced an ambitious regeneration scheme that aims to renew Limerick's troubled housing estates both physically and socially.

The plan is for more than 2,000 houses to be demolished and replaced by new homes for existing residents. There will be a mixture of private and local authority houses and schemes will be made available for local authority tenants to buy their homes at affordable prices.

People with persistent criminal records may be banned from the new houses and people involved in anti-social behaviour may have their social welfare withdrawn. If children vandalise property or do not attend school, their parents may be penalised.

Moyross will be given a new town centre, a railway station, a multi-purpose sports arena and a business park. Improved social facilities ranging from better health services to children's 'homework clubs' will also be provided. Two major garda stations, to house a total of 100 gardaí, will be built in Moyross and Southill.

5 Read the news extract in Figure 2 before answering the questions below.

(a) Name three suburbs of Limerick that will benefit from the urban renewal scheme described in the extract.

(i) _____

(ii) _____

(iii) _____

Name two problems that some residents of these suburbs have had to endure.

(i) _____

(ii) _____

(b) Describe some ways in which the urban renewal scheme described will improve *housing*, *law and order* and *social facilities*.

- *Housing* _____

  _____

  _____

- *Law and order* _____

  _____

  _____

- *Social facilities* _____

  _____

  _____

(c) Suggest one useful thing that an urban renewal scheme could do, but that is *not* mentioned in the extract.

_____

_____

★ **1** Look at the photograph and then answer these questions.

(a) Name one city you have studied which has shanty towns.

_____

(1 mark)

(b) Name and describe three problems for people living in shanty towns.
(9 marks)

- _____

   _____

   _____

- _____

   _____

   _____

- _____

   _____

   _____

Marking Scheme
(a) One (Third World) city named = *1 mark*
(b) Three problems at 3 marks each = *9 marks*
   Allocate each 3 marks as follows:
   Problem named = *1 mark*
   Two points of description = *1 mark + 1 mark*

Most of the answers to the clues in this crossword can be found in Chapters 46, 47 and 48 of your textbook.

Clues Across

1. The growth of cities.
5. Their presence or use leads to crime in Irish cities.
9. Rearrange 'SLAGNIF' to spell a North Dublin suburb.
11. A New Town in Munster.
12. Craigavon is a _ _ _ Town, like 11 across.
16. In Kolkata, people who occupy land 'illegally'.
17. Opposite to rural.
18. One solution to inner city decay.
21. Once called Calcutta.
22. Are bustees *planned* or *unplanned*?
23. Big urban area in the north-west fringe of Dublin.

Clues Down

2. Shanty towns in India.
3. Schools, water supplies, etc. are examples of *infrastructural* _ _ _ _ _ _ _ _.
4. Kolkata is in this country.
6. '_ _ _ism' – a bias against other peoples that leads to crime.
7. Fatima Mansions are situated in Dolphin's _ _ _ _.
8. Once a village, now part of Dublin.
10. Mentioned in Clue 7 down.
13. Urban _ _ _ _ _ _ _, another solution to inner city decay.
14. Ireland's Primate city.
15. '_ _ _ _ _ _ _ _ people' live on Kolkata's streets.
19. New Town near Dublin.
20. When urban areas spread widely and rapidly – urban _ _ _ _ _ _.

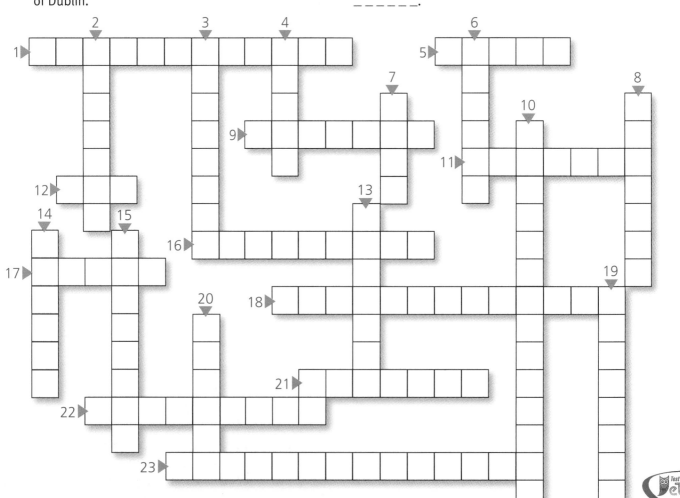

1 Fun Activity

Use this diagram to help you decide whether each of the professions listed below is involved in a primary, secondary or tertiary activity.

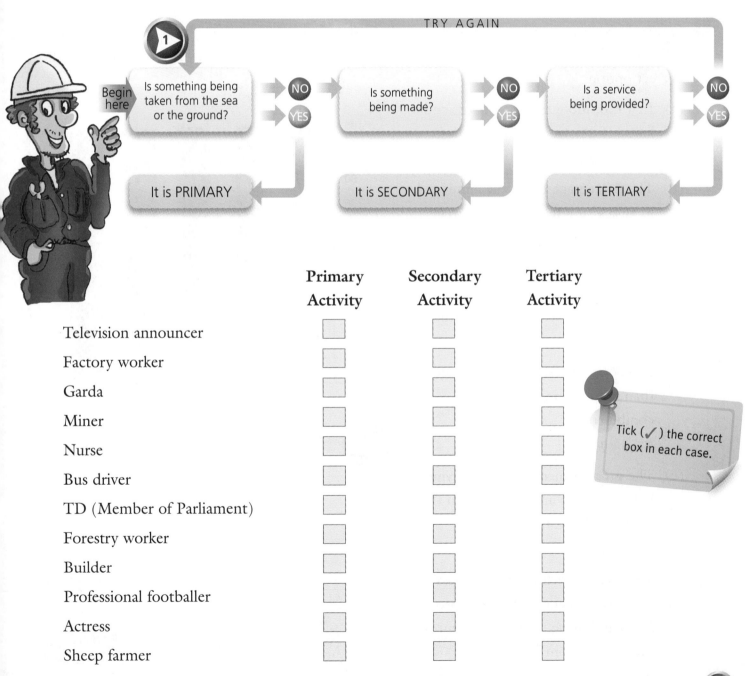

TRY AGAIN

Begin here

Is something being taken from the sea or the ground? → NO → Is something being made? → NO → Is a service being provided? → NO

YES / YES / YES

It is PRIMARY   It is SECONDARY   It is TERTIARY

	Primary Activity	Secondary Activity	Tertiary Activity
Television announcer	☐	☐	☐
Factory worker	☐	☐	☐
Garda	☐	☐	☐
Miner	☐	☐	☐
Nurse	☐	☐	☐
Bus driver	☐	☐	☐
TD (Member of Parliament)	☐	☐	☐
Forestry worker	☐	☐	☐
Builder	☐	☐	☐
Professional footballer	☐	☐	☐
Actress	☐	☐	☐
Sheep farmer	☐	☐	☐

Tick (✓) the correct box in each case.

★ **2** Which of the following lists represent people who *all* work in tertiary activities?

    (a) Farmer, pop singer, teacher, truck driver   ☐

    (b) Banker, factory worker, nurse, chimney sweep   ☐

    (c) Potter, hairdresser, miner, professional footballer   ☐

    (d) Shopkeeper, taxi driver, refuse collector, priest   ☐

★ **3** In the following list circle the *three* jobs that are in the primary sector.

baker	coalminer	computer manufacturer
doctor	farmer	fisherman
shipbuilder	shop assistant	tourist guide

4 Figure 2 shows percentage employment in Ireland in agriculture, industry and services between 1926 and 2006. Indicate whether each of the following statements is *true* or *false* by circling the correct option.

    (a) In 1926, more than half of Ireland's labour force worked in agriculture.

        True / False

    (b) The percentage of people employed in agriculture fell steadily between 1926 and 2006.

        True / False

    (c) By 2006, 10 per cent of the Irish labour force worked in agriculture.

        True / False

    (d) In 1966, services employed more than industry and agriculture combined.

        True / False

    (e) The greatest increase in employment between 1926 and 2006 was in the secondary sector.

        True / False

    (f) The tertiary sector employed less than 40 per cent of the workforce in 1926 and more than 60 per cent of the workforce in 2006.

        True / False

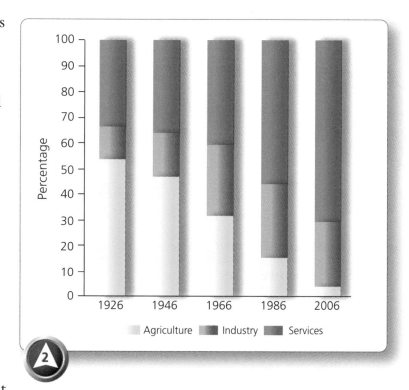

50

1 The graphs in Figure 1 show the daily amounts of water used for different purposes by two different families. One family lives in Dublin, the other in a rural area of India.

The statements 1 to 5 below relate to Figure 1, but not all of these statements are true.

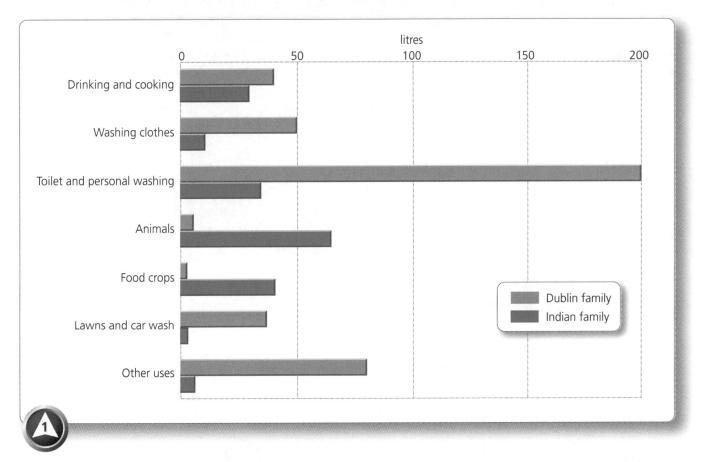

1

1 The Dublin family uses much more water than the Indian family.

2 The Dublin family uses 40 litres more each day for washing clothes than the Indian family.

3 'Toilet and personal washing' accounts for more than 50 per cent of all water used.

4 The Dublin family uses five times more water in the 'toilet and personal washing' category than the Indian family.

5 The graphs suggest that the Indian family is involved in agriculture.

The correct statements are:

1, 2, 4 ☐   1, 2, 5 ☐   1, 3, 4 ☐   2, 3, 5 ☐   *Tick (✓) the correct box.*

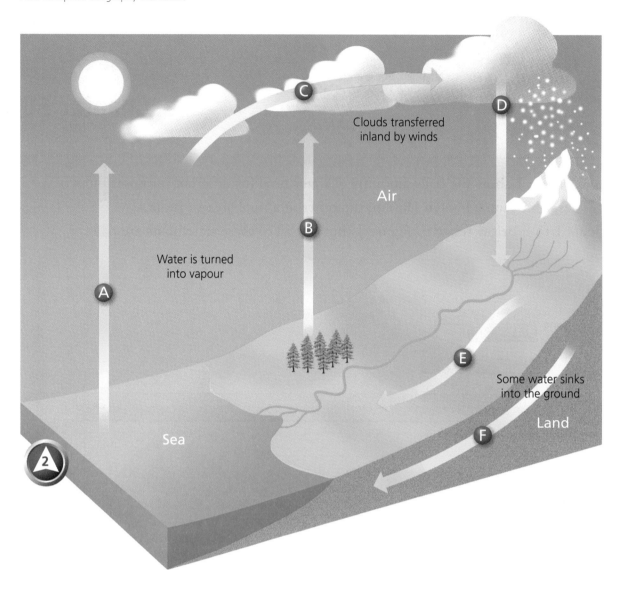

2 Link each of the labels A to F in Figure 2 with its matching statement in Figure 3. One match has already been made for you.

Labels	Statements
C	**Condensation** – water vapour changes to cloud
	Soakage
	Surface water or **run-off**
	Evaporation from seas, lakes and rivers
	Precipitation – rain, sleet, snow, etc.
	Transpiration from plants

★ **3** With the help of Figures 2 and 3, describe the water cycle.
In your answer refer to the terms used in the diagram.

_____

_____

_____

_____

_____

_____

_____

_____

4 Water is an example of a renewable natural resource. In the spaces below list the **renewable and non-renewable natural resources** hidden in the wordsearch in Figure 4.

Funtime!

Each **shaded** box marks the beginning of a word.

S	E	D	I	T	X	B	F	E	K	S	U	T	W	H	G	D	U	L	T
W	T	Z	I	V	R	G	A	H	R	J	V	W	I	G	P	I	T	P	S
C	P	T	M	O	I	D	I	C	N	Q	M	X	N	I	T	R	V	U	K
C	L	U	N	R	A	L	O	S	P	O	L	Y	D	L	W	O	D	P	K
C	X	U	B	C	H	A	T	W	X	Y	Y	Z	N	M	V	N	V	S	V
X	C	O	P	P	E	R	K	I	J	Q	P	O	A	N	T	O	R	X	R
I	Y	W	T	U	V	G	H	F	L	R	R	N	Z	O	Q	R	X	U	T
S	T	X	A	B	C	J	I	G	M	S	M	E	B	P	O	E	T	M	S
T	A	Z	R	S	Q	P	A	E	W	T	A	N	A	Q	P	R	T	I	U
S	H	S	I	F	N	H	D	C	B	V	U	I	C	T	C	N	C	N	T
E	D	G	X	F	M	C	U	O	A	G	Z	G	D	R	Y	S	O	N	N
R	E	K	E	L	O	T	J	I	B	Y	X	B	X	S	X	U	A	I	N
O	H	H	J	I	P	F	I	L	X	A	C	I	J	T	W	C	O	A	L
F	G	F	G	O	L	D	L	H	G	F	D	E	Y	U	V	C	K	N	Z

Renewable

Non-renewable

1 Select *some* words from the selection box to fill in the blanks in 'The story of oil and gas' below.

The Story of Oil and Gas

Oil – the world's most used fossil fuel – is a _____ source of energy. Rich countries of the First World or the _____ use more and more fossil fuels each year, much of it in the form of _____, which is a secondary source of power. Not only is the over-use of oil contributing to _____; it contributes also to occasional large oil spills which _____ our seas so horribly.

The world's leading single producer of oil is _____. Oil has brought riches and prosperity to this country, which was once populated mainly by _____. But because the oil will run out one day, producer countries must use their wealth to _____ their economies while they can.

Oil is extracted by a process called _____. Ireland does not extract oil, but we exploit medium-sized _____ deposits in the Kinsale Field beneath the _____ Sea off the coast of County Cork. Deposits have also been found in the Corrib Field off the coast of County _____, though they are not yet being exploited. Kinsale Gas is extracted and brought ashore by a _____ company called Marathon. It is then sold to _____, which distributes it throughout the country. Some is used for town supplies and some is used to generate electricity at _____.

Selection Box

- nomads
- An Bord Gais
- uranium
- fertilisers
- Clare
- multinational
- Mayo
- Aghada
- diversify
- drilling
- Athlone
- global warming
- Irish
- concentrate
- gas
- quarrying
- pollute
- electricity
- Saudi Arabia
- North
- Celtic
- Japan
- non-renewable
- South
- renewable

2 Indicate whether each of the following statements is true or false by circling the *True* or *False* option in each case.

(a) Poor countries, where most people live, use most of the world's energy reserves. *True / False*

(b) Oil, gas and coal are all sources of non-renewable energy. *True / False*

(c) It is expected that the world's oil reserves will eventually become exhausted (used up).

True / False

3 Examine the labels **A–H** on the map in Figure 1, and the list of features below. In the boxes provided, write the labels that match the features.

Features:

☐ Celtic Sea

☐ Corrib Gas Field

☐ Kinsale Head Gas Field

☐ Oil reserves off Waterford

☐ Gas-fuelled electric power station

☐ Cork–Dublin pipeline

☐ Inter-connector pipeline with Britain

☐ Unfinished or planned pipeline

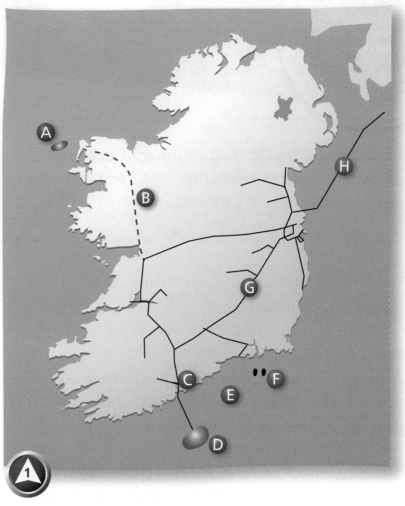

1

4 In the boxes provided, name the types or sources of energy described below. Indicate also whether each energy type of source is renewable or non-renewable.

Description	Type of energy	Renewable or non-renewable
• An energy source that is very plentiful in Saudi Arabia		
• An energy that uses the sun to produce power		
• An energy source exploited off the coast of Co. Cork		
• A secondary source of energy		——

★ 1 Which **three** of the following are extractive industries?

forestry   software industries   peat harvesting   watch making
furniture making   coalmining

- _____   - _____   - _____

★ 2 Which of the following resources is renewable?

oil ☐   hydroelectricity ☐   coal ☐   peat ☐   *Tick (✓) the correct box.*

3 Selecting technology

In the appropriate spaces in Figure 1 write the names of implements and machines used in the past and at present to prepare and harvest Irish bogs and to transport peat. Choose the names of these implements and machines from the selection box.

OPERATION	IMPLEMENTS AND MACHINES	
	... used in the past	... used in the present
• Preparing the bog		• _____ • _____
• Harvesting the peat	• _____	• _____ • _____ • _____ • _____
• Transporting the peat	• _____	• _____

①

Selection Box

- harvester • miller • turf train • ditcher • ridger • grader • harrow • animal-drawn cart • slean

Junior Certificate Higher Level Question with Marking Scheme and Sample Answer

★ **4** (a) *'The use of technology has speeded up the rate of exploitation of Irish peat lands.'*
The diagram in Figure 2 below shows the stages in the exploitation of a bog.
Use the diagram to explain three ways in which technology has been used to exploit the bogs. *(9 marks)*

Stages in the exploitation of a bog

Stage 1	Stage 2	Stage 3	Stage 4
The bog is drained	Peat is harvested	Peat is transported	Peat is marketed

1 _____
_____
_____

2 _____
_____
_____

3 _____
_____
_____

Marking Scheme

Three explanations each score *3 marks* as follows:
- Statement = *2 marks*
- Development = *1 mark*

Sample

A ditcher (**2 ✓**) digs a network of drains in the bog. These drains allow the bog to become dry enough to work on. (**✓ +1**)

(b) *'In the future, Bord na Mona may use cutaway bogs for wind farms.'*
Suggest **three** advantages of cutaway bogs for the location of wind farms. *(6 marks)*
OR
Suggest **three** other ways in which cutaway bogs might be used in the future. *(6 marks)*

1 _____
_____

2 _____
_____

3 _____
_____

Marking Scheme

Three points each score two marks as follows:
- Statement = 1 mark
- Development = 1 mark

133

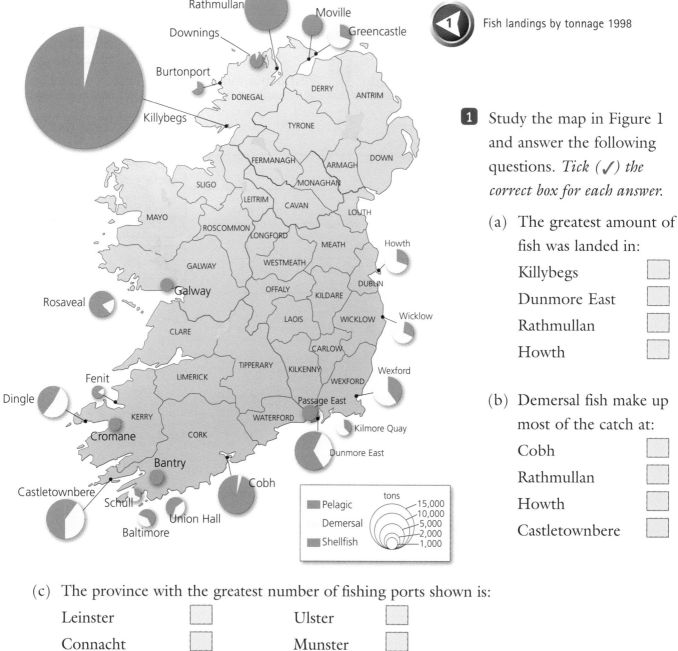

Fish landings by tonnage 1998

1 Study the map in Figure 1 and answer the following questions. *Tick (✓) the correct box for each answer.*

(a) The greatest amount of fish was landed in:

Killybegs ☐

Dunmore East ☐

Rathmullan ☐

Howth ☐

(b) Demersal fish make up most of the catch at:

Cobh ☐

Rathmullan ☐

Howth ☐

Castletownbere ☐

(c) The province with the greatest number of fishing ports shown is:

Leinster ☐   Ulster ☐

Connacht ☐   Munster ☐

(d) A fishing port with landings of less than 5,000 tonnes is:

Wexford ☐   Rathmullan ☐

Kilmore Quay ☐   Rosaveal ☐

2 Depletion of a natural resource

The table of figures shows change over time in herring catches in part of the Celtic Sea off Ireland. (*Catch given in thousands of tonnes*)

Year	Annual Catch*	Year	Annual Catch*	Year	Annual Catch*
1970	26.7	1980	6.3	1990	12.2
1971	24.9	1981	6.4	1991	11.9
1972	23.4	1982	6.8	1992	13.7
1973	22.6	1983	7.1	1993	10.4
1974	19.3	1984	7.5	1994	8.2
1975	17.2	1985	7.9	1995	7.6
1976	13.6	1986	10.0	1996	6.2
1977	11.0	1987	11.7	1997	6.0
1978	10.7	1988	12.0	1998	6.5
1979	6.7	1989	11.0	1999	6.6

★ (a) To what extent does the table of figures in Figure 2 show that fish stocks have been depleted over time in part of the Celtic Sea? (*6 marks*)

Marking Scheme

(a)
- Statement = *2 marks*
- Reference to a year and catch to support statement = *2 marks*
- Reference to another year and catch to support statement = *2 marks*

(b) Three reasons at *2 marks* each. Allocate each *2 marks* as follows:
- Statement = *1 mark*
- Development = *1 mark*

★ (b) Describe three reasons for the depletion of fish stocks in Irish waters. (*6 marks*)

Write **one extra** development for each reason.

3 Use the information in Figure 3 to complete the bar graph in Figure 4 and the line graph in Figure 5.

Year	Catch in tonnes
1965	12,000
1975	29,000
1985	48,000
1995	6,000
2002	22,000

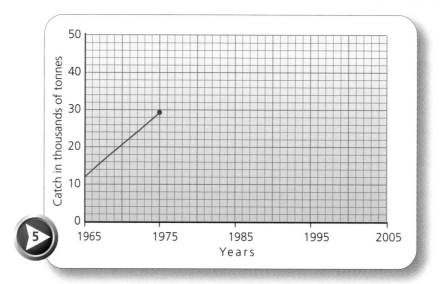

4 Describe three ways of controlling sea fishing so as to preserve Irish fish stocks.

- _____
- _____
- _____

1 Tick the boxes provided to indicate whether each of the items listed below is a farm input, a farm process or a farm output. Some items might be inputs *and* outputs.

	INPUT	PROCESS	OUTPUT
• Tractor	☐	☐	☐
• Ploughing	☐	☐	☐
• Milk	☐	☐	☐
• Feeding animals	☐	☐	☐
• Silage	☐	☐	☐
• Farm buildings	☐	☐	☐
• Manure	☐	☐	☐
• EU grants	☐	☐	☐
• Wool	☐	☐	☐
• Keeping farm accounts	☐	☐	☐

2 The table in Figure 1 shows the land area taken up by different crops in an Irish mixed farm. This information is also represented in the pie chart in Figure 2 below.

Complete the pie chart by writing in the names of the crops in the correct spaces.

Crop	Grass	Barley	Potatoes	Turnips	Other
% of land area used by crop	55	25	10	3	7

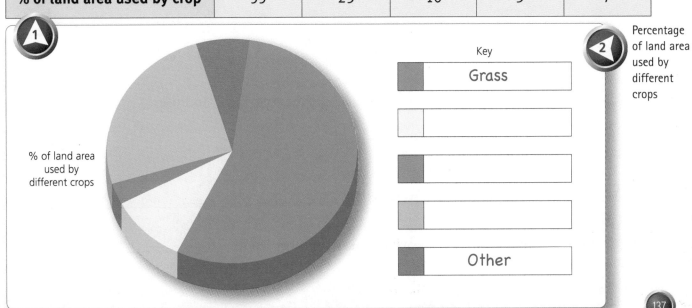

① % of land area used by different crops

② Percentage of land area used by different crops

Key
Grass

Other

3 Figure 3 shows production in a mixed farm in Leinster. Examine Figure 3 and answer the questions that follow.

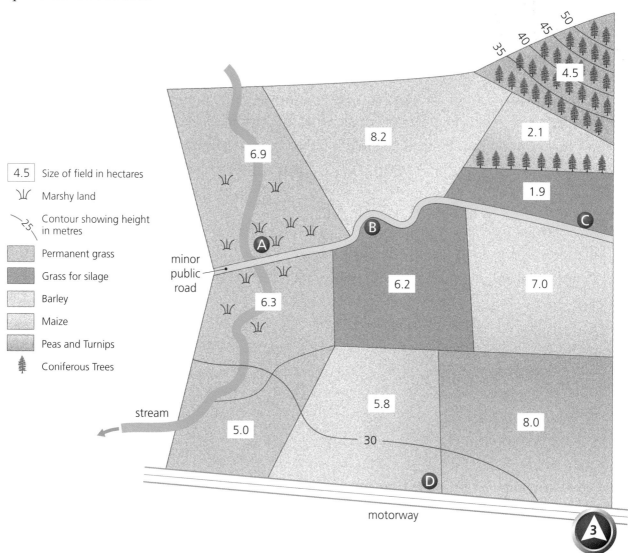

(a) The size of this farm in hectares (ha) is:

45.7 ha ☐   61.9 ha ☐

67.2 ha ☐   73.0 ha ☐   *Tick (✓) the correct box.*

★ (b) How many hectares are devoted to each of the following land uses?

(i)   Permanent grass _____

(ii) Barley _____

(iii) Maize, peas and turnips together _____

★ (c) Of the *tillage* crops shown, which takes up most land? _____

(d) The pie chart in Figure 4 shows the *percentage* of land taken up by each of the crops in the farm in Figure 3. In the box provided, write the percentage of land taken up by coniferous trees.

(e) Do you think coniferous trees are a suitable land use for the field of 4.5 hectares?
Explain your answer.

_____

_____

_____

Maize
13

Barley
24

Grass for silage
13

Peas and
Turnips
13

Permanent grass
30

Coniferous Trees

4

(f) A river flows through the farm in Figure 3.
In which general direction does it flow?

_____

(g) Imagine that it is proposed to build a farmhouse on this farm at *one* of the four locations labelled **A** to **D** in Figure 3.
(i) Identify which of the four locations you would choose and say why.

_____

_____

(ii) For each of the other three locations, state one reason why you would *not* choose that location to build a farmhouse.

• _____

• _____

• _____

(h) Which of the following might *all* be *outputs* of the farm in Figure 3?

Barley, tractor, chickens, eggs ☐   Potatoes, barley, labour, land ☐

Milk, silage, grass, manure ☐   Farm buildings, calves, silage, wool ☐

Tick (✓) the correct box.

Giant Revision Puzzle

This word puzzle relates to all **primary economic activities** and will help you revise Chapters 49 to 54 of your textbook. **ENJOY!**

Clues Across

2. These nets hang like curtains in the water.
5. A primary activity.
6. Another primary activity.
8. Part of the water cycle – rain.
10. Sea between Ireland and Britain.
11. These are part of any system.
14. This machine might be an input in an Irish farm.
15. To give birth. Refers to fish.
16. Equipment used on trawlers to locate other objects.
17. Unusually long period of dry weather.
22. Oil corporation at the centre of the Corrib gas dispute.
24. Saudi _ _ _ _ _ _.
26. Money needed to run a farm or any other business.
28. The _ _ _ _ _ cycle.
29. Energy provided by the sun.
30. Something that goes a full circle – as in the water

    _ _ _ _ _.
31. Machine used to scrape milled peat from a bog.

Clues Down

1. Non-renewable resources are also called this.
3. Process to bring water to dry land.
4. These are part of any system.
6. Oil corporation that developed Kinsale Head Field.
7. Energy source found at Kinsale Head Field.
9. Energy that can be used again and again.
12. Equipment used to locate fish.
13. Gas field off Co. Mayo.
18. Type of net used to scoop fish from near seabed.
19. Used by EU to limit quantities of fish caught.
20. Isle of _ _ _ is in the Irish Sea.
21. The North _ _ _ _ _ _ _ is between Ireland and Scotland.
22. Region on southern margins of the Sahara Desert.
23. River from which South Dublin gets its water supply.
25. A clean and renewable source of energy.
27. This source of power is provided by the sea.

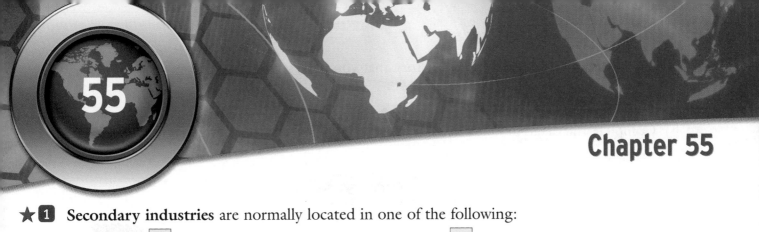

Chapter 55

★ **1** **Secondary industries** are normally located in one of the following:

a garage ☐   an office block ☐

a farm ☐   a factory ☐

★ **2** In the following list, circle the three jobs that are in the **secondary sector**.

baker	coalminer	computer manufacturer
doctor	farmer	fisherman
shipbuilder	shop assistant	teacher

★ **3** Link each term in column X with its matching pair in column Y.

	Column X
A	Activities within a factory
B	Things with inputs, processes and outputs
C	An input into all Irish factories
D	Outputs of some factories
E	An input into a brewery

	Column Y
1	Electricity
2	By-products
3	Barley
4	Systems
5	Processes

X	Y
A	
B	
C	
D	
E	

4 Indicate whether the following statements are *true* or *false*.
(Circle the correct alternative in each case.)

(a) In factories, finished products are processed into raw materials.   *True / False*

(b) Factory buildings, workers and capital are all inputs of factories.   *True / False*

(c) The place where outputs are sold is referred to as 'the market'.   *True / False*

(d) The outputs of some factories can be the inputs of other factories.   *True / False*

(e) Hard disks, motherboards and monitors are all inputs in the *PC Pro*   *True / False*
computer factory.

(f) 'Burn-out' is the name given to a 12-hour test-run period for new computers.   *True / False*

5 (a) Give the name and location of a factory that you have studied.

_____

(b) Complete the diagram below to show some inputs, processes, outputs and other aspects of the factory you named in (a) above.

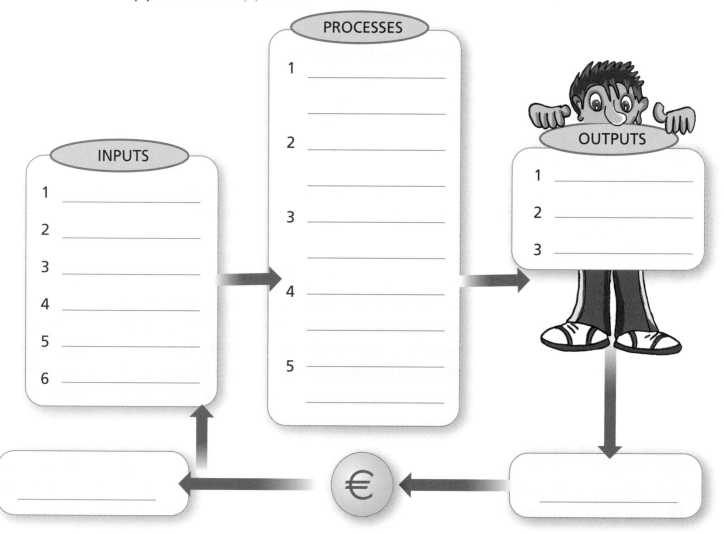

(c) Suggest one local benefit and one benefit to the country of the factory that you named in (a) above.

- *Local benefit*: _____

_____

_____

- *Benefit to the country*: _____

_____

_____

1 The statements 1 to 6 below relate to the photograph given of an Irish Cement factory near Drogheda. Not all of the statements are correct. Identify the correct statements by ticking the correct box below.

1. The factory shown is a typical example of footloose industry.

2. The factory shown is an example of heavy industry.

3. The factory shown is a system with inputs, processes and outputs.

4. Factories such as the one shown are usually located close to their heavy and bulky raw materials.

5. Factories such as the one shown are always branch plants of transnational corporations.

6. This factory would process light raw materials into small, expensive products.

The correct statements are:

1, 2 and 3 ☐   1, 3 and 5 ☐

2, 3 and 4 ☐   3, 4 and 6 ☐

Tick (✓) the correct box.

Irish Cement plant near Drogheda

2 Link each of the letters in Column X with its matching number in Column Y.
One match has been made for you.

	Column X
A	Heavy manufacturing
B	Light manufacturing
C	Shipbuilding
D	Printing
E	'Southside', Togher
F	Footloose industry
G	Limestone, shale, gypsum
H	Infrastructure

	Column Y
1	Example of light industry
2	Uses heavy, bulky raw materials
3	Location of industrial estate in Cork
4	Example of heavy industry
5	Can locate in many areas
6	Water supplies and other services
7	Inputs in cement manufacturing
8	Uses less bulky raw materials

A	2
B	
C	
D	
E	
F	
G	
H	

Junior Certificate Higher Level Question
with Marking Scheme

★3 **Question**: What is an industrial estate? Describe one advantage of building a factory in an industrial estate. *(8 marks)*

_____

_____

_____

_____

_____

_____

_____

_____

_____

Marking Scheme
- What is an industrial estate? = *4 marks* allocated as follows:
  State = *2 marks*
  Development = *1 mark*
  Another development = *1 mark*
- One advantage = *4 marks* allocated as follows:
  Statement = *2 marks*
  Development = *1 mark*
  Another development = *1 mark*

Junior Certificate question with marking scheme and sample answer.

★ **4** **Question**: In relation to a named example of a manufacturing industry you have studied, explain how these three factors have influenced the location of industry: transport; labour; and access to raw materials. *(10 marks)*

Sample Answer

The PC Pro (**2✓**) computer factory is an example of an industry.

1 The factory is situated just off Cork's N28 South Link road. (**2✓**) This allows workers to travel easily to and from work at the factory. (**✓+1**)

2 PC Pro is situated near a large urban labour force. (**2✓**) University College Cork provides graduates who have specialised in electronics. (**✓+1**)

3 Light raw materials are imported through nearby Cork Airport. (**2✓**) Heavier goods are imported through Ringaskiddy port. (**✓+1**)

Marking Scheme

Named industry = *1 mark*
Three factors at *3 marks* each.
Allocate each *3 marks* as follows:
- For transport:
  Statement = *2 marks*
  Development = *1 mark*
- For labour:
  Statement = *2 marks*
  Development = *1 mark*
- For access to raw materials:
  Statement = *2 marks*
  Development = *1 mark*

Now answer the same question using another named manufacturing industry that you have studied. Use the marking scheme given.

Name of industry: _____

- *Transport:* _____

  _____

  _____

- *Labour:* _____

  _____

  _____

- *Access to raw materials:* _____

  _____

  _____

1 Complete the passage below by circling the correct *alternatives* and by choosing words from the Selection Box to fill in the gaps.

Selection Box

- Lancashire
- oil
- twentieth
- industrialisation
- cut down
- Teeside
- charcoal
- Weald
- exhausted
- Sheffield
- steel
- subsidies
- Yorkshire
- Port Talbot
- iron
- ore

Industries may change their location over time. Some industrial areas decline, while others experience a growth of industry or _____. This happened in the case of the Irish / British iron and _____ industry.

Britain's earliest iron works used _____ as a source of power. They were therefore located near great forested areas such as The _____ and the Forest of Bean / Dean. Another advantage of these early locations was that they contained rocks that were rich in _____ ore. It can be said, therefore, that Britain's earliest iron industry was a market based / resource-based industry.

By the year 1600 / 1800, most of Britain's forests had been _____. Coal / Iron ore then became the dominant source of power and Britain's iron and steel industry moved to isolated / coalfield locations such as those in South / North Wales, in L_____ and in Y_____.

The final great move in Britain's iron and steel industry was from the coast / coalfields to the coalfields / coast. This happened from the middle of the _____ century. By that time, Britain's coal and iron _____ reserves had become almost _____. In any case, coal was being replaced by _____ as a source of power and this new energy source had to be imported into Britain by air / sea. It was more convenient, therefore, to replace Britain's old iron and steel works with new mills near the coast / mountains. The new steel mills were located in places such as _____ in Wales and _____ in North-east England.

****

Not all industry changed location. Industrial decline / inertia caused some industries to remain where they were. Steel making in _____ is a good example of industrial inertia. Steel making survived there because of the area's great reputation for making cheap / top quality steel, such as is used in the making of surgical / agricultural instruments. In any case, a great deal of money had been spent modernising Sheffield's steel plants. Some of this had been spent by the British government, which offered _____ to the Sheffield steel industry to help reduce unemployment / immigration in Britain's Midlands / West Coast.

Chapter 58

★ 1 Study the table in Figure 1 and then circle the correct answer in *each* of the statements below:

Type of employment	Males	Females
Farming, fishing and forestry	89,086	7,193
Manufacturing (factory) workers	182,306	42,714
Building and contruction workers	133,961	2,737
Office work, managing and government workers	114,726	203,839
Commercial and sales	121,627	118,288
Service workers	69,564	101,014
Communication and transport workers	92,488	9,956

1

(a) More *males / females* are 'service workers'.

(b) More *males / females* work in 'farming, fishing and forestry'.

(c) More females work in '*commercial and sales*' / '*manufacturing*'.

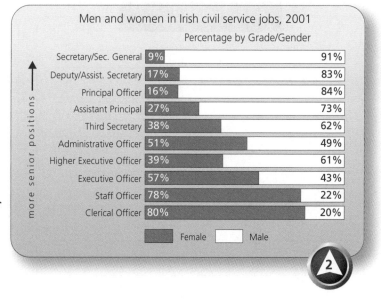

2 The statements below refer to the information in Figure 2. Indicate which of the statements are true or false by circling the correct *True / False* alternative in each case.

(a) The more senior positions are occupied mainly by men.   *True / False*

(b) Most female civil servants occupy less senior positions.   *True / False*

(c) Females dominate the four least senior positions shown.   *True / False*

(d) Women hold less than one-fifth of each of the three most   *True / False*
senior positions shown.

(e) The percentage of female employees declines steadily   *True / False*
from the most senior to the most junior positions.

.

3 Which statement best describes the situation shown in the cartoon?

men and women do the same work ☐   more women still do lower-paid jobs ☐

men and women are paid the same ☐   more women than men are managers ☐

★ **4** *The role of women in industry has changed over time.*
Discuss the above statement in relation to Ireland and to China.

Ireland	China

148

★ **1** The table in Figure 1 shows the employment structure for a country. Examine Figure 1 and use the information in it to fill the spaces in the three statements given below.

	Sector	1981	1988	1993	2002
% in employment	Agriculture	16	13	10	7
	Manufacturing industry	26	23	23	25
	Services	48	48	50	63
% of labour force unemployed		10	16	10	5

In 2002 the percentage employed in **agriculture** was _____ per cent.

In 1993 the percentage employed in **services** was _____ per cent.

In 1981 the percentage of the labour force that was **unemployed** was _____ per cent.

2 Which of the pie charts in Figure 2 – A or B – represents the employment situation in 2002 shown in the table in Figure 1?

Pie chart A ☐   Pie chart B ☐

primary   secondary   tertiary   unemployed

3 Describe briefly and give two examples of each of the following: *Examples*

- Industrialised countries _____

  _____   • _____

  _____   • _____

- Newly industrialising countries _____

  _____   • _____

  _____   • _____

- Industrially emergent countries _____

  _____   • _____

  _____   • _____

149

4 The map in Figure 3 shows countries, not by their actual shapes or sizes, but according to the size of their industrial outputs in 1996. The statements below relate to Figure 3. Identify which of the statements are correct.

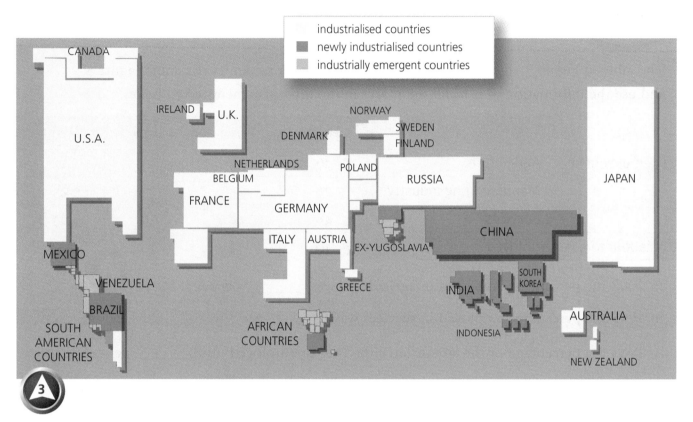

1. Russia had a greater industrial output than all EU states combined.

2. The countries with the largest industrial outputs were the USA and Japan.

3. The UK had a larger industrial output than that of all of Africa.

4. Ireland's industrial output was less than that of Greece.

5. The continent with the least industrial output was Africa.

The correct statements are:

1, 3 and 4　☐　　　　2, 3 and 4　☐

2, 3 and 5　☐　　　　3, 4 and 5　☐　　　*Tick (✓) the correct box.*

5 Name one advantage and one disadvantage of the kind of map shown in Figure 3.

● *Advantage:* _____

● *Disadvantage:* _____

1 The flow chart in Figure 1, when complete, will show how acid rain is formed. Select the four **correct statements** from the list given below and place them in the **correct order** to fill each of the blank boxes in Figure 1.

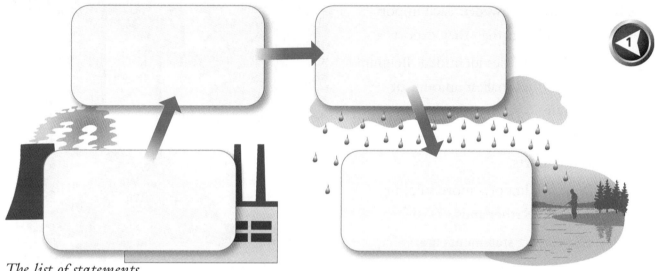

The list of statements

- Precipitation causes the gases to fall as acid rain.
- Motor vehicles, hydroelectric stations, etc. produce fossil fuels.
- The gases evaporate as harmful acid rain.
- Sulphuric oxide and nitric dioxide gases are released into the air.
- The gases combine with moisture and become acids.
- Fossil fuels, such as coal and oil, are burned.
- Sulphur dioxide and nitrogen oxide gases are released.

2 Link each of the terms in column X with its matching pair in column Y.

Column X	
A	Have been severely leached by acid rain
B	Is used as a measure of acid rain
C	Has had its surface damaged by acid rain
D	A German area that has been damaged by acid rain
E	Are a major cause of acid rain
F	Is a major producer of acid rain

Column Y	
1	The Colosseum
2	The United States of America
3	Motor vehicles
4	pH value
5	Soils
6	The Black Forest

A	
B	
C	
D	
E	
F	

3 Figure 2 shows a selection of European countries that 'import' and 'export' harmful sulphur through the prevailing winds. The following statements relate to Figure 2. Only some statements are true. Identify the true statements by ticking the correct box.

A. Britain is the biggest exporter of sulphur.

B. Norway and Sweden each import more sulphur than they export.

C. Of the countries identified, Belgium exports the smallest amount of sulphur.

D. Italy exports twice as much sulphur as it imports.

E. Denmark imports more sulphur than the Netherlands.

The correct statements are:

A, B, D ☐   A, C, D ☐

A, D, E ☐   B, C, D ☐

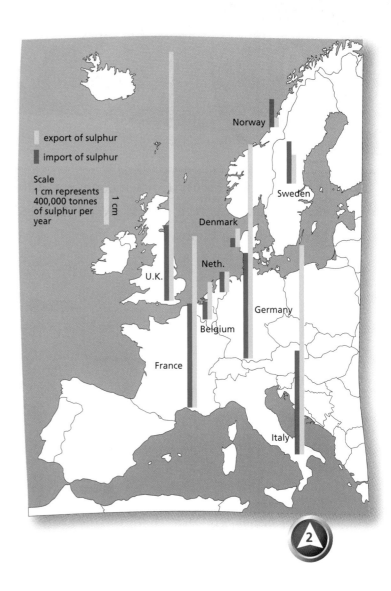

4 Identify three ways in which acid rain can damage a country's economy.

(a) _____

(b) _____

(c) _____

5 Suggest two ways of reducing acid rain.

(a) _____

(b) _____

1 Examine the **OS map of the Cork area** on page 176 of your **textbook**. Imagine that there is a proposal to build a large pharmaceutical (medicines) factory between Ballyphehane and Grange, which is situated at W 685 693 on the map.

★ (a) In the box provided, draw a labelled sketch map to show the location of the proposed factory.

★ (b) Give two arguments that local people might use *in favour* of and two arguments that local people might use *against* the location of the new factory in the area proposed.

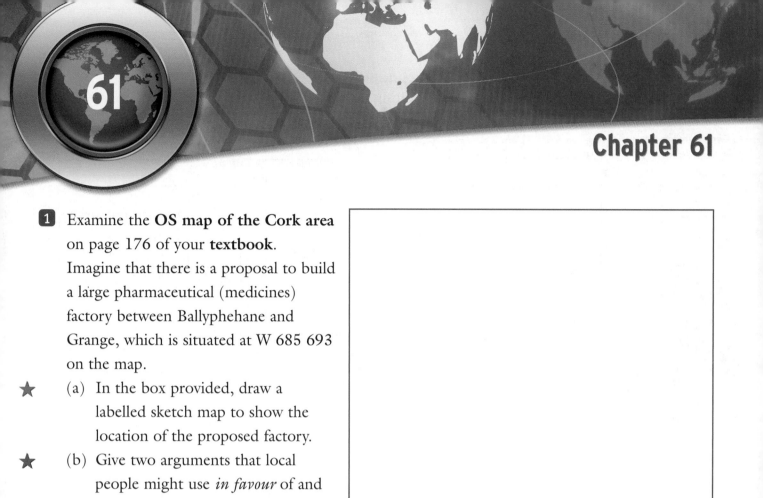

Arguments in favour	Arguments against
• _____ _____ _____ _____ • _____ _____ _____ _____	• _____ _____ _____ _____ • _____ _____ _____ _____

Word Puzzle

Enjoy this **revision word puzzle** on manufacturing industry

The *number in brackets* after each clue gives the textbook page on which the answer can be found.

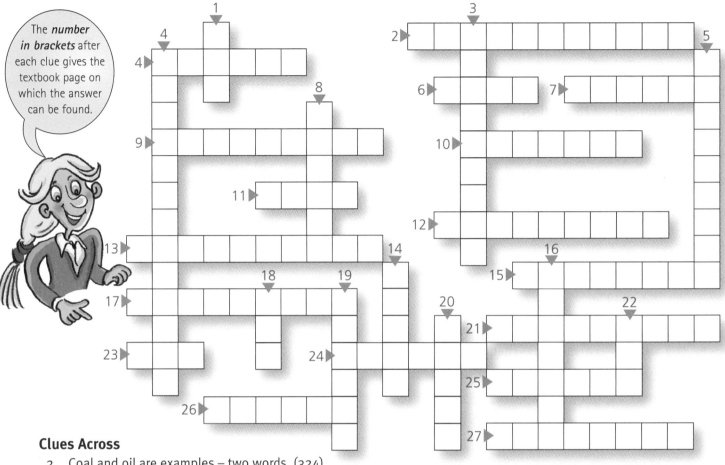

Clues Across

2. Coal and oil are examples – two words. (324)
4. The place where industrial outputs are sold. (310)
6. An industrially emergent country in South America. (322)
7. Factor affecting the location of industry – sounds like a political party. (308)
9. Factor affecting industrial location. Could include roads, rail, etc. (308)
10. Location of major steel plant in North-East England. (315)
11. Was famous for German coal. (312)
12. Type of government in China since 1949. (320)
13. EU _ _ _ _ _ _ _ _ _ _ Funds have helped to build roads in Ireland. (311)
15. Some factories benefit from these connections with nearby firms. (310)
17. An industry that can be situated successfully in many places. (312)
21. Fine steel is made at this English location. (316)
23. Fossil fuel (324)
24. This Port makes steel in Wales. (315)
25. Acid fog can cause this illness. (325)
26. _ _ _ _ _ _ *Processing Zones* have been set up in China. (321)
27. Acid rain can increase this soil process. (325)

Clues Down

1. Iron _ _ _ is the main resource material for steel making. (314)
3. A factory with extremely bad working conditions. (321)
4. A company with factories in many countries. (306)
5. Activities within a system that turn inputs into outputs. (303)
8. PC Pro is situated in this part of Cork City. (304)
14. The _ _ _ _ _ was an ancient centre of iron and steel making in England. (314)
16. Industrial _ _ _ _ _ _ _ might discourage a factory from moving to another location. (316)
18. Today's most used fossil fuel. (324)
19. Light industry might be located in an industrial _ _ _ _ _ _. (307)
20. A little animal or part of a computer. (304)
22. Industrial Development Authority. (311)

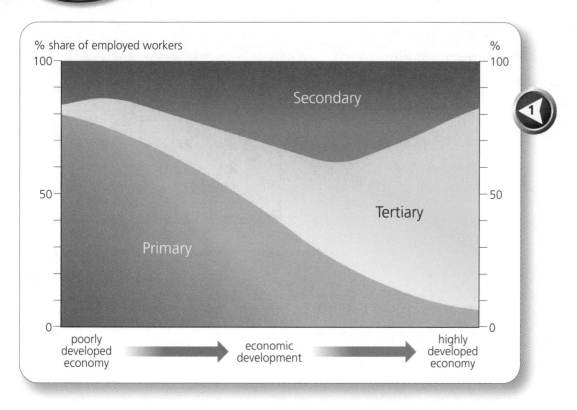

1. Figure 1 shows changes in the importance of primary, secondary and tertiary activities as the economy of a country develops.

The following statements relate to Figure 1. Indicate whether each statement is true or false by circling the *True* or *False* alternative.

(a) Eighty per cent of workers in the poorly developed economy are employed in primary activities.   *True / False*

(b) As an economy develops, secondary activities continue to grow steadily in importance.   *True / False*

(c) In the highly developed economy, more than 90 per cent of workers are employed in tertiary activities.   *True / False*

(d) The highly developed economy is dominated by service activities.   *True / False*

(e) Primary activities decline in importance and tertiary activities increase in importance as an economy develops.   *True / False*

★ 1 Look at the bar graph (Figure 1) showing the number of tourists who visited a historic building in a year. The largest number visited the building in:

February ☐

April ☐

August ☐

December ☐

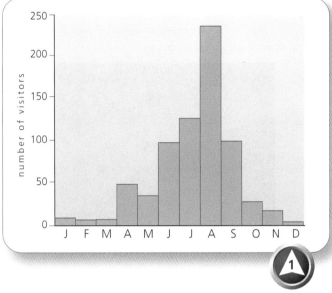

2 Look again at Figure 1. Attempt to explain briefly why July and August were the busiest months.

● _____

● _____

★ 3 Examine Figure 2, which shows spending on recreation as a percentage of household spending.

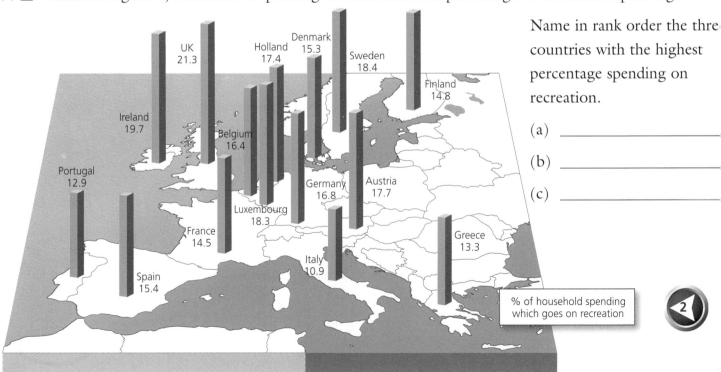

UK 21.3
Holland 17.4
Denmark 15.3
Sweden 18.4
Finland 14.8
Ireland 19.7
Belgium 16.4
Portugal 12.9
Germany 16.8
Austria 17.7
Luxembourg 18.3
France 14.5
Greece 13.3
Spain 15.4
Italy 10.9

% of household spending which goes on recreation

Name in rank order the three countries with the highest percentage spending on recreation.

(a) _____

(b) _____

(c) _____

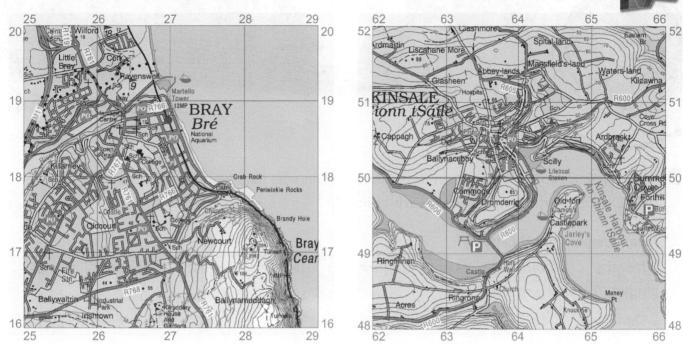

4 Examine the *OS map fragments above* showing the coastal resorts of Bray (Co. Wicklow) and Kinsale (Co. Cork).

(a) In the boxes below, indicate the presence or absence in each of the resorts of the tourist attractions/facilities listed below.

Attraction/Facility	Bray	Kinsale
● Sandy beach	✓	✗
● Sheltered harbour		
● Boating activities		
● Caravan park		
● Camp site		
● Youth hostel		
● Tourist information		
● Antiquities		
● Easy access		

> Place a tick (✓) in the appropriate box to indicate the presence of a facility. Place a cross (✗) to indicate the absence of a facility. One example has been done for you.

(b) In which of the two resorts shown would you prefer to take a holiday?
Give one reason for your answer by referring to evidence from the map only.

Resort: _____

Why: _____

_____

1 With reference to the information in Figure 1 explain why Lanzarote would be a better choice than Dublin for the location of a 'beach holiday'.

Mean temperature (° Celsius)

Months	April	May	June	July	August	September	October
Dublin	14°C	15°C	16°C	18°C	20°C	16°C	12°C
Lanzarote	18°C	23°C	26°C	30°C	32°C	25°C	20°C

Hours of bright sunshine

Months	April	May	June	July	August	September	October
Dublin	5	6	5.5	5	6	4	3
Lanzarote	7	9	10	11	10	7	5

Climatic data for Dublin and Lanzarote (Canary Islands)

Junior Cert Marking Scheme
- *Two explanations* needed at *5 marks each.*
- **For each explanation** give:
  a statement *(2 marks)*
  a development *(2 marks)*
  another development *(1 mark)*

You must use the climatic data supplied to score more than *3 marks* in each explanation.

- _____
  _____
  _____
  _____
  _____

- _____
  _____
  _____
  _____

Junior Certificate Higher Level Question with Marking Scheme

★A *'Climate makes some regions attractive to tourists.'*

Examine the graphs given in Figures 2 and 3, which show the precipitation and temperature figures for a popular tourist region in Europe. Answer the questions that follow.

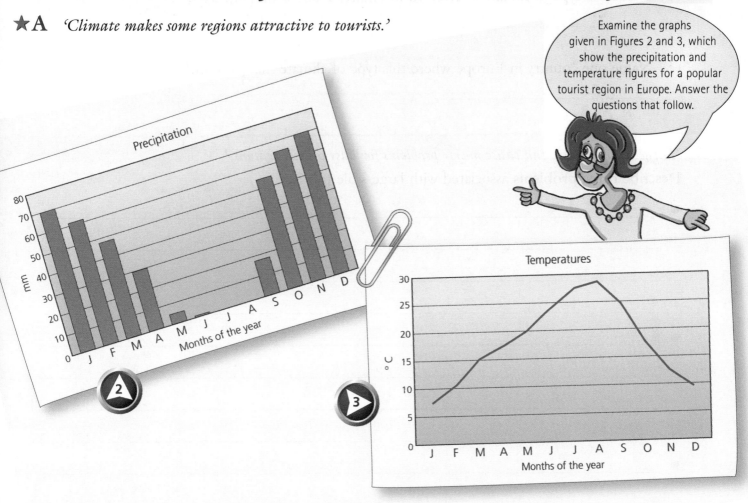

(a) Describe two ways in which the climate shown would attract tourists.

- _____
  _____
  _____
  _____
  _____

- _____
  _____
  _____
  _____

The rest of the question and the marking scheme are on page 160.

(b) Name the type of climate referred to in Figures 2 and 3 on page 159.

_____

(c) Name one country in Europe where this type of climate may be found.

_____

B *'Large-scale tourism can cause major problems for busy tourist regions.'*
Describe **three problems** associated with large-scale tourism.

- _____
_____
_____
_____

- _____
_____
_____
_____

- _____
_____
_____
_____

Marking Scheme

Question A

(a) Two explanations at *4 marks* each. One explanation must refer to precipitation and the other to temperature.
Allocate each *4 marks* as follows:
- Statement = *2 marks*
- Development referring to graph = *2 marks*

(b) Name type of climate = *1 mark*

(c) Name one country = *1 mark*

Question B

Three problems at *4 marks* each. Allocate each *four marks* as follows:
- Statement = *2 marks*
- Development = *2 marks*

1 Which three of the statements below best reflect the message of the cartoon in Figure 1?

1. Poor countries need assistance from developed countries.

2. Most African people migrate to Europe and the USA to use up the surplus goods produced there.

3. Most people live south of the Equator.

4. The North produces more goods than it needs.

5. The wealth of the world is very unevenly distributed.

6. Many people in the South look in the wrong place for things.

The statements that best reflect the cartoon are:

1, 2 and 3 ☐   1, 2 and 4 ☐   1, 3 and 5 ☐

1, 4 and 5 ☐   2, 3 and 4 ☐   3, 4 and 6 ☐   *Tick (✓) the correct box.*

	Country A	Country B
Primary sector	80	5
Secondary sector	5	25
Tertiary sector	15	70

2 The percentages of working people engaged in primary, secondary and tertiary economic activities in two countries

2 (a) Use the statistics in Figure 2 to complete the bar graphs in Figure 3.

(b) Use the information in Figure 2 *and/or* Figure 3 to fill in the blanks and to circle the correct alternatives in the passage below.

Country A represents a *slowly developing /developed* country. Its economy is dominated by _____ activities, such as *banking /trading /farming*. Fewest people are engaged in the _____ sector, which employs only *one tenth /one twentieth* of working people. This country could be *China /Uganda*.

Country B represents a *quickly developing /developed* country such as *the USA /India*. Most people in this country work in the _____ sector, which employs *more than / almost* three-quarters of workers. Both _____ and _____ activities are more important in country B than they are in country A. But the _____ sector in country B employs only five per cent of the workforce.

(c) Explain what is meant by '*a quickly developing country*'.

_____
_____
_____
_____
_____

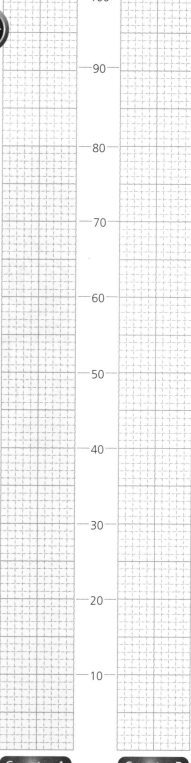

3

Country A   Country B

Primary Sector
Secondary Sector
Tertiary Sector

1 Tick (✓) the correct box to answer each of the following questions.

A colonial power was:

(a) A system by which one country controlled other countries ☐

(b) A country that was a colony of another country ☐

(c) The 'ruling' country in an Empire, together with its colonies ☐

(d) A country that controlled other countries as colonies ☐

In colonial trade, colonies:

(a) Usually exported manufactured products and imported raw materials ☐

(b) Usually exported raw materials and imported manufactured products ☐

(c) Usually exported raw materials at high prices ☐

(d) Usually imported manufactured products at low prices ☐

2 Use the grid to link each number in Column X with the match of its letter in Column Y.

Column X	
1	Former colonial power
2	Former colony
3	Plantation in Ireland
4	Landlords
5	The Great Famine
6	Cash crops

Column Y	
A	had many tenants
B	Britain
C	1845–1849
D	grown for money
E	land confiscated
F	Egypt

X	Y
1	
2	
3	
4	
5	
6	

★ **3** Figure 1 refers to aspects of trade between powerful and poor countries. Examine the cartoon and read the statements relating to it. Not all of the statements are true.

1. Poor countries receive little for their exports but pay dearly for their imports.

2. International trade favours powerful countries at the expense of poor countries.

3. International trade benefits both powerful and poor countries equally.

4. Many poor countries export raw materials and import manufactured products.

The true statements are:

1, 2, 4 ☐   1, 2, 3 ☐

1, 3, 4 ☐   2, 3, 4 ☐   *Tick (✓) the correct box.*

4 Figure 2 shows changes in the values (prices) of a selection of manufactured products and a selection of primary products between 2002 and 2008.

Selected Manufactured Products (with a 2002 base value of 100 units)	Year	2002	2003	2004	2005	2006	2007	2008
	Value	100	108	120	132	140	148	160
Selected Primary Products (with a 2002 base value of 20 units)	Year	2002	2003	2004	2005	2006	2007	2008
	Value	20	28	16	18	12	22	16

Use the statistics in Figure 2 to complete the two line graphs in Figure 3.

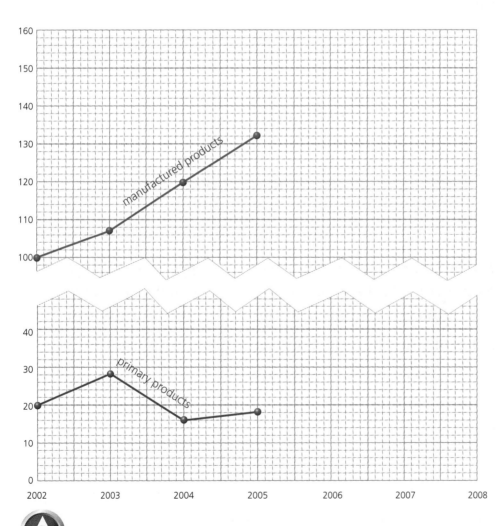

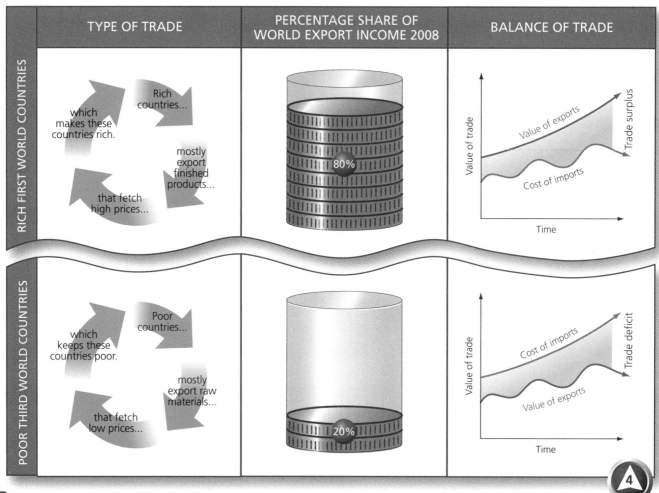

TYPE OF TRADE	PERCENTAGE SHARE OF WORLD EXPORT INCOME 2008	BALANCE OF TRADE

RICH FIRST WORLD COUNTRIES

Rich countries... mostly export finished products... that fetch high prices... which makes these countries rich.

80%

Value of trade — Value of exports — Cost of imports — Trade surplus — Time

POOR THIRD WORLD COUNTRIES

Poor countries... mostly export raw materials... that fetch low prices... which keeps these countries poor.

20%

Value of trade — Cost of imports — Value of exports — Trade deficit — Time

4

5 Figure 4 shows how trade affects many First World and Third World countries.

(a) Use the information in Figure 4 to fill in the blanks and circle the correct alternatives in the passage below.

Rich First World countries mainly export *raw materials / finished products* that fetch *high / low* prices on the world market. This makes these countries _____. Furthermore, rich countries receive a _____% share of the world's export income. They have trade *deficits / surpluses* because the value of their _____ is greater than the cost of their _____.

(b) Use the information in Figure 4 to describe *three problems* that world trade causes for poor Third World countries.

- _____
  _____
- _____
  _____
- _____
  _____

Test Yourself eTest.ie

★ **1** Use the information in Figure 1 to complete the partly finished bar graph in Figure 2.

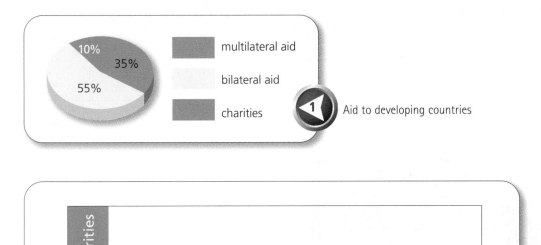

2 In the boxes provided, match each letter in Column X with the number of its pair in Column Y. One pair has been completed for you.

	Column X
A	Aid given by the government of Ireland to the government of Ethiopia
B	Something that is cultivated for sale
C	Aid given through organisations such as the United Nations
D	Medicine, shelter and food
E	Aid with conditions attached
F	An Asian country that receives Irish aid
G	An African country that receives Irish aid

	Column Y
1	Bilateral aid
2	Tied aid
3	Emergency aid
4	Cash crop
5	Multilateral aid
6	Uganda
7	Vietnam

X	Y
A	
B	
C	
D	
E	
F	
G	6

★ **3** The picture below shows the victim of a *tsunami* (huge tidal wave) in Asia.

(a) Describe the type of aid that the people shown in the picture will need immediately. (*5 marks*)

_____

_____

_____

(b) Describe the type of aid that will be needed for future development. (*5 marks*)

_____

_____

_____

Marking Scheme
Allocate each *5 marks* as follows:
● Statement = *2 marks*
● + development = *2 marks*
● + another development = *1 mark*

★ **4** In the space provided name *three* Irish non-governmental aid organisations (NGOs) that support development in Africa.

(a) _____

(b) _____

(c) _____

5 The **bar chart** in Figure 3 shows actual Irish international aid in millions of euro between 1996 and 2008. The **line graph** shows Irish international aid as a percentage of Irish GNP during the same period. The statements (a)–(c) below relate to Figure 3. Indicate whether each statement is true or false by circling the *true* or *false* options.

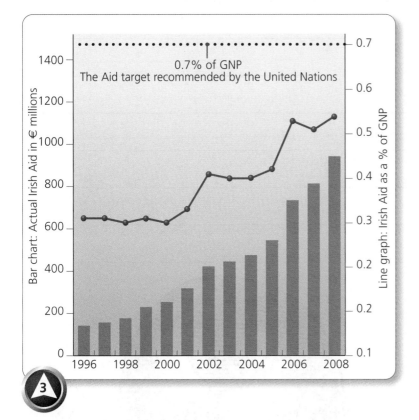

(a) Actual Irish aid was highest in 1996 and lowest in 2008.

True / False

(b) In 2006 Ireland gave more than €700 million in aid.

True / False

(c) Ireland has not yet reached the percentage aid target of the UN.

True / False

6 Which set of selections (a) to (d) given below represents the correct combination of African countries shaded in Figure 4?

(a) Mali, Mozambique, Lesotho, Ethiopia ☐

(b) Zambia, Mali, Kenya, Ethiopia ☐

(c) Ethiopia, Zambia, Tanzania, Mali ☐

(d) Ethiopia, Lesotho, Tanzania, Niger ☐

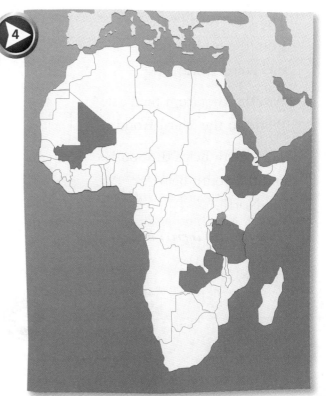

7 **How good are Irish Aid Programmes?**

Evaluate Irish Aid programmes to the Third World. Make four points and mention specific examples of Irish aid.

● _____

_____

● _____

_____

● _____

_____

● _____

_____

8 Which of the following messages does the **cartoon** give?

The North gives aid
to the South.   ☐

The First World benefits
from the exploitation
the Third World.   ☐

Wealth flows from the First
World to the Third World. ☐

The North helps the South
and the South helps
the North.   ☐

Tick (✓) the correct box.

WORLD TURNED UPSIDE DOWN...

1 In the boxes provided, match each of the terms in Column X with its matching pair in Column Y. One match has been completed for you.

Column X	
A	Capital city of Sudan
B	Large area suffering from desertification
C	A western region of Sudan
D	A country to the west of Sudan
E	A country to the south of Sudan

Column Y	
1	Darfur
2	Uganda
3	Khartoum
4	The Sahel
5	Chad

X	Y
A	
B	
C	
D	
E	

2 (a) Name four developmental problems faced by Sudan, which are referred to in the extract in Figure 1.

(i) _____

(ii) _____

(iii) _____

(iv) _____

(b) Name one problem, not mentioned in the extract, which hinders development in Sudan.

_____

_____

Crisis in Darfur
(from a document by Concern)

Over one million people have been forced to flee their homes in war-torn Darfur, Sudan. People have left with nothing, having seen their villages burned and looted and their livestock stolen.

These people are now in great danger from hunger and disease in the crowded camps to which they have fled. This area of Africa suffers from severe drought. But the rainy season of recent weeks now means that families are crammed together in muddy and unhygienic conditions and are at serious risk from waterborne diseases such as cholera.

A quarter of children under the age of five are already weak from malnutrition – making them particularly vulnerable to disease.

The destruction of homes, crops and livestock means that families have nothing to return home to and will be affected by the crisis for a long time to come.

Junior Certificate Question with Marking Scheme

3 Explain two ways in which war and the spending of money on arms have prevented economic development in one named developing country of your choice.

(*10 marks*)

Named country: _____

- **Sample explanation**: Millions of Sudanese have been killed or injured in civil wars. (✓ **2**)

  Many of the injured people cannot work again. (✓ **2**) _____

- _____

  _____

  _____

- _____

  _____

  _____

4 Which **three** of the following statements relate best to the message or the messages given by the cartoon in Figure 2? Circle the three statements of your choice.

(a) It is always windy in the Third World.

(b) There is too much 'military aid' and not enough emergency aid.

(c) War improves food supplies.

(d) Spending on arms is harming human development.

(e) Poor people need bread, not weapons.

Development Snakes and Ladders

(To play and think about.)

56	57 Unjust world trade	58	59	60 Famine	61 WIN
55 International debt cripples economy	54	53	52 EU funds new farming scheme	51	50	49
42	43 Land is redistributed among poor people	44	45	46 Civil war in Darfur	47	48
41	40 Prices of exports collapse	39 Bilateral aid increases	38	37	36 Better health education	35
28 Foreign banks reduce loan charges	29	30	31	32 Big country invades weaker country	33	34
27	26	25 Drought in Sahel	24 Fair trade helps Third World	23	22 AIDS kills millions	21 Birth rates fall
14	15 United Nations offers help	16	17	18 'Military aid' from rich nations	19	20
13	12	11	10	9	8 Improved status of women	7
BEGIN	1	2	3	4 Trocaire sends help	5	6

Regional Incomes Per Head (in Euro) 1969–2004		
Region	**1969**	**2004**
Border	6,880	21,260
Midland	6,652	21,219
West	6,598	21,778
TOTAL BMW (BORDER MIDLAND WEST)	**6,728**	**21,440**
Mid-West	7,823	23,329
South-West	8,183	22,618
South-East	7,865	20,774
Mid-East	7,513	22,954
Dublin	11,120	26,229
TOTAL S+E (SOUTH AND EAST)	**9,103**	**23,869**

①

1 Use the information given in Figure 1 to indicate whether each of the following statements is true or false. (Circle the *True* or *False* alternative in each case.)

(a) In 2004, the total South and East (S+E) region had a higher income per head than the total Border Midland West (BMW) region. *True / False*

(b) The total BMW region had a per head income of €6,728 in the year 2004. *True / False*

(c) The BMW region and the S+E region are each made up of three smaller sub-regions. *True / False*

(d) The Dublin sub-region had a higher per head income than had the Mid-West sub-region. *True / False*

(e) The total S+E region had a per head income of more than €20,000 in 2004. *True / False*

(f) Each region and sub-region shown had a higher per head income in 2004 than it had in 1969. *True / False*

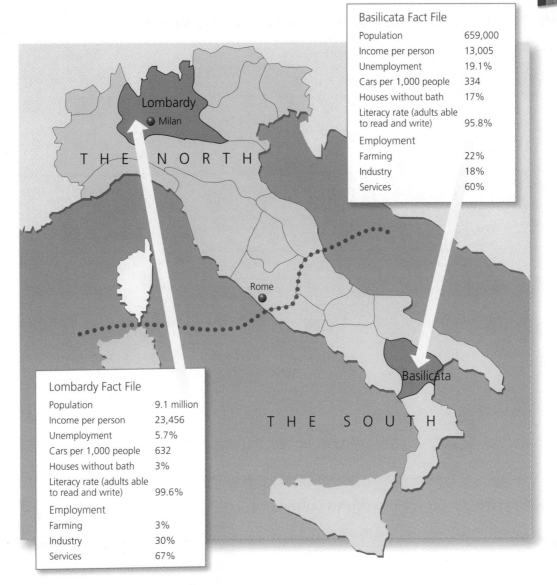

Basilicata Fact File

Population	659,000
Income per person	13,005
Unemployment	19.1%
Cars per 1,000 people	334
Houses without bath	17%
Literacy rate (adults able to read and write)	95.8%
Employment	
Farming	22%
Industry	18%
Services	60%

Lombardy Fact File

Population	9.1 million
Income per person	23,456
Unemployment	5.7%
Cars per 1,000 people	632
Houses without bath	3%
Literacy rate (adults able to read and write)	99.6%
Employment	
Farming	3%
Industry	30%
Services	67%

2 *'Places such as Lombardy in Northern Italy are generally more prosperous and economically developed than are places such as Basilicata in Southern Italy.'*

Use the information in Figure 2 to show that the above statement is true. Make four different points. Include in each point a statistic relating to Lombardy and a statistic relating to Basilicata.

- _____
  _____

- _____
  _____

- _____

★ **3** Study the map, which shows some richer and poorer regions in Europe.

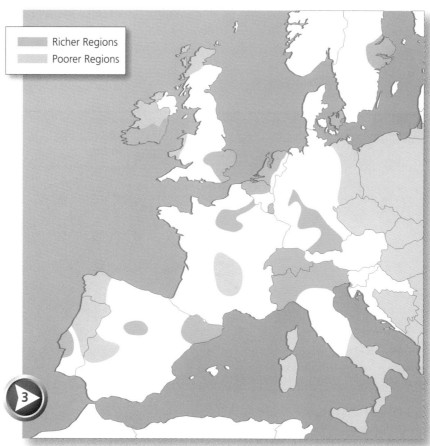

Richer Regions
Poorer Regions

(a) Name **two** poorer regions shown on the map.

● _____

● _____

(b) In the case of **one** of the named poorer regions, describe **two** reasons why it is poor.

Marking Scheme

(a) Two regions named @ *1 mark* each = *2 marks*

(b) Two reasons = *4 marks*
Allocate each *4 marks* as follows:
Statement/reason identified = *2 marks*
Two developments @ *1 mark* each = *2 marks*

● _____

_____

_____

_____

_____

● _____

_____

_____

_____

_____

70

1. Examine Figure 1. Then indicate whether each of the statements below is true or false by circling the *True* or *False* option.

   (a) People in the Third World benefit greatly from First World aid.

   True / False

   (b) The First World does little or nothing to help the Third World.

   True / False

   (c) What the First World gives in aid it takes back by means of debt repayments and trade.

   True / False

2. First World and Third World people sometimes disagree about how inequality between North and South should be reduced. In the spaces provided, summarise two possible 'First World solutions' and two possible 'Third World solutions' to global inequality.

   First World solutions

   (a) _____

   _____

   _____

   _____

   (b) _____

   _____

   _____

   _____

   Third World solutions

   (a) _____

   _____

   _____

   _____

   (b) _____

   _____

   _____

   _____

Fairtrade and Gregoria Vargas

Gregoria Vargas is a great supporter of the international organisation called *Fairtrade*. Gregoria is a small coffee grower from Peru, South America, and *Fairtrade* has given her and her family their first chance ever of earning a decent wage.

For years Gregoria and people like her have been exploited by the powerful multinational companies and the greedy middlemen who control most of the coffee trade in Third World countries.

Now Gregoria sells her crop directly to *Fairtrade* and that has made all the difference. *Fairtrade* treats small coffee-growers as partners to be respected, rather than as weak people to be cheated. The organisation pays steady and fair prices for the coffee it buys and insists that decent working conditions be provided for coffee-labourers. *Fairtrade* even pays their suppliers some money in advance, so that poor coffee producers do not have to seek loans from greedy moneylenders.

Delicious *Fairtrade* coffee, tea and other products, can now be bought in many cafes in Ireland, as well as in supermarkets and charity shops. Look out for the *Fairtrade* logo! By buying *Fairtrade*, you too can play a small but important role in reducing inequality in the world.

3 Outline three ways in which *Fairtrade* helps small coffee producers.

* _____

* _____

* _____

Mention one way in which you and your classmates might be able to help small-scale coffee producers in the Third World.

_____

_____

The Junior Certificate Examination

The Layout of Junior Certificate Examination Papers

In order to do well in your Junior Certificate Geography examination, it is very important that you *manage* your examination correctly. To do this you will need to know the layout of the examination paper.

> **Both the Higher Level and Ordinary Level examinations:**
> - Are allocated two hours.
> - Carry a total of 150 marks.
> - Contain two main sections.
> - Require you to answer all questions from Section 1 and any three questions from Section 2.

Section 1 of the Examination
- This section contains 20 '**short questions**', all of which should be answered.
- These questions relate to all parts of the course and many are accompanied by graphs, tables of figures or other inputs.
- Section 1 carries a total of **60 marks** (3 marks for each short question), which is 40 per cent of the total marks for the examination.

Section 2 of the Examination
- This section contains five questions, any **three** of which must be answered.
- Each question has several parts and is likely to cover topics from different areas of the course.
- In recent years, one question in the Higher Level examination and two questions in the Ordinary Level examination have related to the Ordnance Survey map and the aerial photograph that accompany the examination paper.
- Section 2 carries **90 marks** (30 marks for each of three questions), which is 60 per cent of the total marks for the examination.

Tips and Tactics

✓ At the beginning of the examination, **read** each question very carefully. Make sure you understand the questions that you intend to answer.

✓ Always **answer 'on the point'** of the questions asked.

✓ If questions relate to graphs, maps or other **inputs,** you should normally refer in your answers to the information given in these inputs.

✓ The **length of your answer** should relate to the number of marks carried by the question.
For example, a question carrying ten marks will require a longer and/or more detailed answer than a question carrying four marks.

✓ Work carefully to a **timetable** in the exam so that you set aside time to **answer all the questions required.**

✓ Always **arrive in good time** for the beginning of the examination and **never leave the examination before it is over.** If you complete the examination with some time to spare, use this time to improve on the answers that you have already written.

A Possible Examination Timetable

It is very important to use a *timetable that suits you* for answering questions in the examination. Below is one *possible* timetable:

✓ **Reading, choosing and highlighting***	**10 minutes**
✓ **Twenty short questions (Section 1)**	**30 minutes**
✓ **Three 'multi-part' questions (Section 2) at 25 minutes each**	**75 minutes**
✓ **'Insurance' time (in case you spend a little too long on any question)**	**5 minutes**
Total time:	***120 minutes***

* **Read** the examination paper, **Choose** the questions from Section 2 that you wish to answer. **Highlight** the key words in these chosen questions.

> The command words with the ***** symbol are those that are used most commonly.

Command Words

Here is a list of 'command words' that you might find in your Junior Certificate examination. It is important that you understand and write 'to the point' of the command words that are given.

General Terms

* Name ...	Give the *name only*, **do not** describe
List ...	Give the *names only* of a number of things
Rank ...	List in order of importance
Rearrange ...	Change the order of
* Describe / discuss ...	
Outline ...	Write an account of
Write a note on ...	
Identify ...	Could mean 'name', as in '*Identify three features of river erosion*'. Could mean 'describe briefly', as in '*Identify three reasons for world hunger*'
State ...	The same meanings as 'say' or 'point out'
Indicate ...	
Calculate ...	Work out exactly
* Examine ...	Look at or study – this term usually relates to a map, photograph, table or diagram
* Explain ...	
Account for ...	Give reasons for
Give the causes of ...	
The effects of ...	The 'results' or 'consequences' of

> When asked to describe, discuss, etc., always do the following:
> 1. Make a clear *statement*.
> 2. *Develop* the statement.
> 3. Mention an *example* if possible.

Compare ...	Give the similarities and/or differences between two or more things
Contrast ...	Give the differences only between two or more things
Compare and contrast ...	Give similarities *and* differences between two or more things
Advantages ...	Good points
Disadvantages ...	Bad points
Define ...	Give a precise but clear meaning of
Write a paragraph on ...	The length of a paragraph should depend on the number of marks allocated to it.
Write a note on ...	Usually the same meaning as 'write a paragraph on'

Regarding maps, photographs or diagrams:

With reference to the map ...	
Using photographic evidence ...	These terms require you to refer to or use a map, photograph or diagram in your answer
Describe with the aid of a diagram ...	
Label ...	These terms require you to show, name and 'arrow point'
Mark and identify ...	certain features, usually on a sketch map or diagram
Insert ...	Write in and label
Locate ...	Give the locations of places on maps or photographs.

Regarding Section 1 of the examination:

* Tick ...	
* Match ...	
* Circle ...	
Cross out (delete) ...	(The meanings of these terms are obvious.)
Complete (the graph, etc.) ...	
Shade in ...	

For permission to reproduce photographs the author and publisher gratefully acknowledge the following:

ALAMY: 3TL, 4, 9TR, 21, 90, 115BL, 11BR, 115BLC, 115TLC, 178;
BRICK: 118, 120, 164, 170, 172, 177; FAIRTRADE: 178; GETTY: 11CR;
IMAGEFILE: 3TR, 8, 9TL, 115TL; IRISH CEMENT: 143;
MARTYN TURNER: 161; PANOS: 123, © Sven Torfinn;
PETER BARROW: 69; PHOCUS: 16, © Keith Heneghan;
PHOTOCALL: 115CL; REUTERS: 168, © Amit Dave.